The Seven Creative Principles

HIRAM E. BUTLER

The Seven Creative Principles, H. E. Butler
Jazzybee Verlag Jürgen Beck
86450 Altenmünster, Loschberg 9
Deutschland

Printed by Createspace, North Charleston, SC, USA

ISBN: 9783849693695

www.jazzybee-verlag.de
www.facebook.com/jazzybeeverlag
admin@jazzybee-verlag.de

CONTENTS:

PREFACE.

These Lectures are published at the particular request of the members of the Society for Esoteric Culture, before which body they were delivered during the spring of 1887; an earnest desire having been unanimously expressed to possess the same in permanent form.

They will be found highly suggestive and valuable to thinking people, on account of the original views presented, and the novel and forcible analysis and treatment of the great subject of Creation.

They contain so many central thoughts that are new to the general public, that, in treating the several Principles, some repetition has been found necessary in the different lectures, on account of the mutual dependence and interrelation of the Seven; but not more than was deemed essential to fully impress and enforce the central facts and workings of Nature.

They are not submitted as labored and polished essays, but rather as gushing springs from the great fountain of natural Truth, to refresh the soul, strengthen the mind, and open the eyes of the spiritually inclined to possibilities of attainments not now thought of.

Editor.

יהוה

" I will be what I will to be."

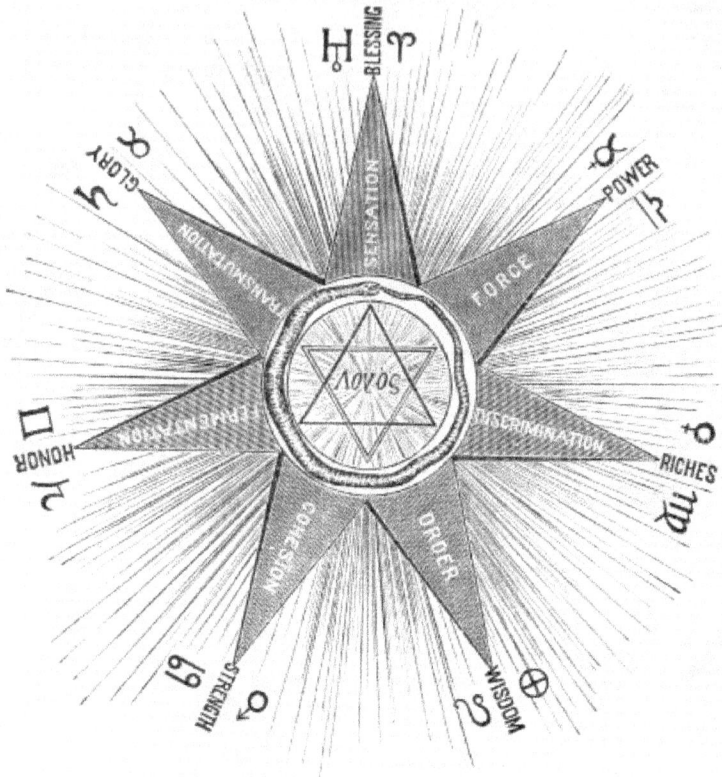

DIAGRAM OF CHART REFERRED TO IN THIS LECTURE.

FIRST LECTURE. THE IDEA OF GOD.

The subject selected for the lecture of this evening is the Idea of God. All religions and all systems of occult science, from the earliest history of the world to the present time, have been characterized entirely by that ideal of God which has been held by the people with whom these systems originated.

The word God in all languages of the world, with perchance the exception of the English, has carried with it the idea of power. In the Hebrew language, for instance, we find, as the expression of the idea, the word El or Elohim, which embodies and expresses the idea of power or almighty creative power; and in all the languages and religions of the world the word selected for the expression of a people's conception of a Supreme Being had for its principal signification the idea of power, — a power that was over and above all, and that was not only power in itself, but the cause and source from whence all manifestations of power emanated.

When scientists search for the prime cause of creative energy, they commence by examining the methods of nature. They observe the growing vegetation, they see the molecules of matter gathered together by the forces of the great mother earth; with the aid of the microscope they trace the formation of these molecules from a stage where atoms are too minute to be discerned, even by the magnifying lens, and arrive at the conclusion, that, from all that is revealed, the process of building matter into form is invariably the same, and that beyond the molecules and atoms that can be discerned there are myriads that are imperceptible, and whose existence can be affirmed only by the unanswerable argument of analogy and logic. The creative force they have thus far been unable to discover, but the result of a creative force is fully manifest, — an interior power that builds and demonstrates, and from which orderly and harmonious structures arise, emblems of an interior and invisible order and harmony, be its source what it may, yet ever orderly and expressive of method and intelligence in its creative manifestations.

The materialistic scientist has usually arrived at the conclusion that matter has in itself the requisite potency to build orderly structures, beyond which he cannot go, and thus is empty of adequate or satisfactory solution of the great problem of life.

In our effort to present to your minds our ideal of God, we shall endeavor to enable you to conceive of a Supreme Being who has attributes much broader and greater than has heretofore been generally accepted. We do this because we believe that in order to attain to the knowledge of grand truths and states of unfoldment one's conception of a great, all-pervading divine essence must embrace the grandest and most ennobling ideal of

3

which human nature is capable. It is only necessary to look into the history of the world to see how closely the character of the nations has been moulded by their ideals of God. The nations which have believed in one or many gods — gods whose principal endowments were those of the worst attributes of human nature; who were vindictive, jealous, constantly warring with each other or with their subjects — modeled their lives in conformity with their belief, justifying their desire for revenge and domination by force, — the strong oppressing the weak b}the power of their own might, — thus honoring and imitating the overbearing, unsympathetic ideal gods of their imagination. Thus we find in all history that according to their ideal of God such has been the character of the people.

Man is of necessity a religious being. The idea of a God has possessed all nations and classes. A people so low down in the scale of unfoldment, who have not had an idea of God — calling it " The Great Spirit," as did the American Indians, or by some other significant name — has never yet been found. Why this should be would be a difficult question to answer, were it not that at the foundation of all being there is a something oftentimes vague and indefinite, but that nevertheless gives a consciousness of an infinite, an over-power, upon which man in his necessities may rely, unto which he may pray or offer sacrifice, propitiate by destroying his enemies, or anger by neglect or scorn of its power.

Scientists tell us that we cannot understand or even think of anything of which we have not some correspondent within ourselves. Thus far we bear them company; but when they state that we can know nothing but that of which the five senses take cognizance, we take issue, for this is far from true. When we speak of cause, which of the material senses perceives or comprehends it? Not one of them can do it! They cannot perceive the commonest principle in nature, which is force! To what does such a materialistic assumption lead? Let us consider. You may feel the weight of the stone that falls upon your hand or person, but do you feel the impelling force? No! Gravity was there before and after the fall of the stone, but you were unconscious of its presence; but when this power takes possession of the inanimate stone and brings it down upon your person, you feel the result of the action, but that which caused the stone to fall you cannot feel. You may see the train of cars whirling along, but that subtle something that has been brought into play by the expansive action of heat, producing the energy which so forcibly propels them, you cannot see: it is beyond the scope of the five senses. Thus you may go over the entire catalogue of moving forms, and you will find that the material senses cannot take cognizance of anything that belongs to cause. This makes it necessary that we should reason from the facts of our observation and experience, and accept the deductions logically resultant therefrom as the obvious truth. Philosophy began, and has expanded, with the effort to determine what is life; and to-night the same problem is before us for consideration, and we still ask, What is life? We see the manifestations of life in the animal world; we observe it in the vegetable domain; we find that even the earth, the rocks, and every existing thing is filled with life, and that all are constantly undergoing change through the unceasing effort of this something we call life. If we endeavor to look beyond this realm of matter, how much can we see? what can we thus learn of life through the agency of the five senses? We turn and investigate the human body; this is the starting-point of the ancient philosophers. They began with the body, and sought inward and upward for the cause, unlike the modern scientist who, commencing with man, traces down and out until he is lost in the intricacies of nature. Let us in our investigations return to the methods of the ancient philosophers, beginning with the highest attribute of man, — the will.

It is by the power of will that we are enabled to move a hand. If a more powerful will takes control of ours, — psychologize us, as we say, — it can prevent us from moving even that, notwithstanding our own will may desire so to do. We know that we cannot move a muscle without the consent of the will. We talk about the involuntary action of the system, but such action is nothing more or less than the movement by the will in accordance with an established habit of being. Every possible action of our organization may, by the effort of our own will, be suspended; and investigation has proved that there are those who are capable of suspending every action or function of the system, even bringing the involuntary activities under control of the will. Thus habit, being induced through the operation either of one's own will or of that of the parent organism, may again be dominated by the same agency. Continued practice causes the hand of the mechanic or musician to act in as regular and systematic manner as do any of the apparently involuntary muscles. I have seen men execute the most intricate mechanical work, that which required the utmost nicety and exercise of fine artistic sense, such as could be attained only by long and untiring application, without any apparent thought or attention. Therefore, we see that the will not only establishes but corrects and controls habits, and is the dominant power and ruler of all.

In our search after God it becomes necessary to look within and beyond. We therefore proceed in accordance with this law in our analysis of the highest form of earthly organization; namely, man. When we have ascertained what man actually is, we begin to form a rational, in fact the highest possible, conception of how and from whence he originated. Let us turn our attention to the old cabalistic name Yahveh, which I have chosen to place on this chart (see diagram) as representing the cause of the seven creative principles, which we shall discuss in subsequent lectures. This (pointing to the chart) is the Hebrew word Yahveh. It occurs over sixty-four hundred times in the Hebrew Bible. It is translated, I think, in our version but four times, in three of which it is rendered as Jehovah, and in the fourth as Jah or Yah; and you will notice in the English translation of the Scriptures, that wherever the name of the Deity is used, when derived from Yahveh, it is invariably spelled with capital letters. This word Yahveh, the cabalistic name for GOD, means, " I will be what I will to be." You will see that this expresses supreme ability and indomitable potency. Who among the sons of men dare step forward and say, " I will be what I will to be "? Think of it! not merely implying, but asserting, that the ability to be whatever lie wills to be exists in himself. Here we have a foundation thought, and here I will say, that in this " I will be WHAT I will to be " we find the key to the whole Hebraic Scripture.

Now let us look and see what a subtle power the will is. We will, and we move; or the will may be excited, and we say that we are angry; and when the will is excited to anger, what a storm exists in the body! how the red blood mounts to the face! every nerve is strained to its utmost tension! what an abnormal strength is called into being to resist and overcome obstacles! And thus even the weakest organizations are by this power of the aroused will enabled to assert and maintain their right (or possibly wrong) at all hazard. Thus you see that the will is the absolute monarch, ruling every muscle and nerve, governing every thought; and that every other power in man is subservient to this king.

Let us look still further, and turn our attention to this planet, earth. It is relatively but a little ball revolving around the sun, its great centre of light. It has eight companions, — yes, more; there is a large family of worlds, each revolving around the same centre, each following in its own prescribed orbit. Here we must become conscious that there is a great power that causes these worlds to revolve around their common centre, each travelling in its defined orbit; and then we find that our centre, the sun, is but a planet of a greater and grander system, and is, with its family of worlds, revolving around another sun; and further still, that this third sun and its family of worlds, is travelling around another sun of a still greater and grander system, so great and grand that it is supposed by some that to complete one revolution consumes over twenty-two and a half million of our years. Here the telescopic deductions of man now cease. But do mathematics cease here? We think not. There are mathematical methods by which it can be proven that all these worlds are born from a great central sun; and that as they are farther and farther removed from it, they become finer and more ethereal, are more fully developed by the same law of transmutation and change that we observe in our planet, the earth; which earth is but an immense electric machine, generating currents of electricity and magnetism which bind it to its sun. The material elements are being transmuted to finer essences of being, and in these worlds born from the central sun we find that they are getting finer and less physically strong in their currents;

6

therefore they are drifting farther away from their centre. If we will investigate our planet, the earth, we shall find that it is becoming finer and less strong physically; that every generation of its inhabitants is becoming more refined than its predecessor. Look back for a few generations, and see what a different character they bore from the people of to-day; how much weaker are we in muscle, how much stronger in brain; how much greater flights of thought are being taken today than in years long ago. Thus thought and mental power are gaining, while physical energy is decreasing. Thought is the co-worker of the will; it is not the will, but is submissive to its power: we think, and consequently act. But there are powers that can overcome the mandates of our will: for instance, let us take electricity. Suppose you take hold of the poles of a strong electric battery, put your will to work and say you will hold it; let a strong current of electricity be turned on, and where is the will? The arms are drawn up, the muscles are contracted, and the will has no power whatever over them. Here is a power that acts like the will, but is much stronger. It is the solid and grosser materials of the decomposing elements of nature, potent with the Divine will, that are throwing off and emitting a current that is stronger than the will of man, and will dominate it in spite of his greatest exertion; if but the necessary mechanism and material is supplied. From the fundamental idea, then, that these worlds are born, grow, unfold, become more and more spiritual, — or, if you should choose a perhaps better word, more mental, — they become more like the Author Mind, the physical energies decrease, they drift farther away from their centre, as their mentality becomes developed so as to enable them to support their existence at a greater distance from the parent sun; and the farther they are removed from their centre of light, the more luminous they become of themselves. As we go farther on, we observe, and shall try to show, that there is no difference between life and light. Taking this as an analogy, then, our earth must of necessity be destined at some far-away period of time to become a central sun, luminous with life and light, from which worlds will be born. It has thus far had but one child born from it, — our moon. The greater planets have greater numbers of worlds born to them, and at some far-away period of the future they will each form a great system, filling their allotted sphere.

We can only discern material substance and things that are like ourselves. As these worlds of which we have spoken become finer, more ethereal, more independent of their sun, they become suns themselves. Changing our line of thought, let us trace from our earth to its central sun, which sun being but a planet, itself revolving around another sun, its centre, — this centre revolving around another sun, its centre, — jet visible, and supposed to be a star in the constellation Pleiades, and we find that we can logically go still farther; but for the material eye to see, the telescope and other appliances for aiding its vision are not yet adequate. We find that we may go on and on, and that each sun, as we come nearer the great centre, is finer and more ethereal. It has been asserted that there is a fourth dimension of matter; something more than length, breadth, and thickness; something that is interior to what we have been considering. As we go on tracing these worlds, finding them to be finer and yet finer, we mathematically conclude that this planet of ours may, at this very moment, be sweeping the interior organization of a far grander world than any of which we have formed the slightest conception, and whose people are refined to such an extent that they have no more consciousness of our existence than we have of theirs. So from mathematical conclusions we may trace until we can conceive the thought that all which we call space is peopled with worlds and systems of worlds, interior to other worlds and systems of worlds, until there shall be no such thing as space; and that in this which we call space we could, were our eyesight sufficiently refined to take cognizance of all the conditions of matter, perceive millions and millions of worlds, interior to still other worlds, all interpervaded by one Great Essence of Being, which, for lack of better terms, we call God, spirit, soul, or life. We are bewildered when we seek to locate cause, and when thus going out in thought into the breadth and vastness of creation we can see that we may logically conclude that this which we call space is so densely filled and inhabited, and not only inhabited, but interinhabited, that it is not space, but is occupied by existing and orderly moving worlds. We can also see that all these systems are governed by a definite law of order. Order pervades everything. Not a plant can grow, not an organic life exist, except by the law of order. We need never expect a machine to be made to do our work except it have form and order. It takes mind to make a machine, and to so construct it agreeably to the law of order that it will perform the work which we design it shall do. If a man should bring to us, perchance, the delicate machinery of a watch, and say, " This grew of itself," could we believe it? Could we possibly believe that the existence of such machinery happened by chance? that the pieces of metallic substance fell down from somewhere, and by some jostling came together in this perfect order? No! nothing could convince us, or any other number of thinking men and women, but what there was a mind, an intelligent and reasoning power, that caused every part to be made, put in its place, and arranged in its order. When we look out upon our world and see how it, and everything in and upon it, is in the most perfect order, can we think that it was formed without intelligence? — much less when we look into our solar system and see its multitude of worlds, each revolving around a common centre, all held in perfect order, all working with the exactness of unparalleled machinery which surpasses the possibilities of the conception of the human mind, can we for a moment think that there is not a mind behind it? that there is not a will that controls it? Certainly not. Now we must pause in the presence of this great, almost unknowable machinery of nature, working in perfect harmony, without inharmonious action in any part.

It has been stated by astronomers that if it were possible for one world to be out of time for a moment, that all systems would be thrown into chaos, so perfect is the law of order in nature. Now there must be a mind and will that is holding everything in its place. There is a thought that has built everything. There is a will that controls all, and that will is like the will which governs the machinery of our bodies. When we get further on in this course of lectures, we will show you that there are reasons for believing that not only is there an intelligent cause, but that this intelligent cause has actually the form of man. The old philosopher and astronomer who gave to us the picture we have in the common almanac of to-day — of the man with the twelve zodiacal signs around him — had a reason for it; and we will show you further that Swedenborg, although considered a dreamer and visionary, agreed exactly with all the visions and prophecies of antiquity; that the planet earth and its inhabitants were all members of one great body, one grand man. These facts are arrived at from the annual revolution of our planet through the four quarters of its ecliptic. These four quarters being again divided into twelve parts, give to us an insight to all the mystic symbols of our Bible, wherein we find the twelve sons of Jacob, the twelve apostles of the Lamb, and the twelve which are so constantly referred to in all the prophecies. These twelve divisions of the ecliptic through which the earth passes, if you will observe them, take for commencement the sign Aries. This sign has reference to the head and power of the reason. The earth enters into this sign of the zodiac on the twenty-first of March. Now if you will take the trouble to examine into the characters of persons who were born when the earth was in this sign, say for one month dating from the twenty-first of March, you will find that they are all persons who demand a reason for everything, are ready to give their own reason for all they bring forward, and are generally inclined to support their reasons in a somewhat logical manner. By thus comparing the character of persons with the indications belonging to each of the twelve signs, you will find that character may be more fully delineated than by any system of phrenology; for these twelve departments of the zodiac actually contain the twelve principles that form the twelve different functions of man, and their centre is the will, which controls the grand man. (This subject is fully treated in my work on " Solar Biology.") We then conclude that the God of the solar system, the power which controls life within the limits of that system, is in the form of man, and works through the grand functions of the solar man. The same evidence teaches us that we may carry the idea of man into the ecliptic through which our sun travels in its revolutions around its centre, and so we may go on eternally and still find the form of man interior to all created suns and worlds, tracing this divine principle yet more and more interior, until the mind is lost in its inquiries into the mystery of what this God-man is. I tell you, friends, that the same law of logic holds good in considering individual man; and when we have solved the question, " What is man? " we have also solved the problem, "What is God?" Man himself has possibilities of godly attributes and powers greater than any that has yet entered into the conceptions of human thought, superior to any that has had being or form on this planet. But what does this bring us to? To this conclusion: that that which we call God, the creator and cause of all things, could, as Swedenborg truly says, " create but from himself."

In our bodies we are limited in creative work to the powers within ourselves. Generation and creation may be used as synonymous terms, for all things have come into existence by generation, formed of the parts and particles of the parent organism. If we trace this to the infinite and unknowable man whom we call God, the great universal man who is the life of all things that exist, where do we come? We reach the conclusion that all that we call matter is only another state of existence of the same Being or Cause. When we have an idea of a spiritual and unseen being that we call God, we, with the ancient cabalists, formulate an idea of a place or state of perfect white light, which light is the source of all fire, but of a fire that is creative, gives life, but destroys nothing. Whatever our idea may be, let us expand it once and for all to this: that the gross matter upon which we walk is but the concentration of the Infinite Spirit. Matter itself is only a condition of spirit, and as that condition changes, it becomes invisible to our perception; and so we may go on, on, eternally on, from state to state interior and yet more interior. What we call solids to-day may tomorrow be changed into gases, pass out of sight. We may call it ether, spirit, mind, or what we will; for the fact that there is nothing known in the universe that cannot be turned into gases and thrown off into what we call space, and no longer have form, measurement, or weight, is in itself evidence that as into this it can be turned, from it it must have come. Then what shall we think of God? What is God? God is everything, is everywhere; fills all space; fills all things; is the life and intelligence of all things; is the motive power of all things. "But," you may say, "you are destroying entirely the ideal we have been worshipping under the name of God." No, no! not at all! For, as we have already said, this idea of God brings you back to the idea of your own being. For you are of God, and God is within you; all that you are, all that you can be, all that you may attain to, is of God; and without the God within you, the essence of the Great Soul of the universe, which animates and inspires you, what would you be? The physical shell, which is the house that contains this great vivifying and all-enlightening spirit, is but a clod of senseless matter, which must soon be resolved into the elements from whence it came.

To enlarge upon this theme: the entire mass of humanity are but parts of one grand whole; each member is but an emanation from the great universal mind, and it takes the whole to make the one great body; and you and I, and our earth, and all that is within it, are members of this one body; hence we cannot injure a single member without injuring the whole body. Therefore, there is true logic in the idea of the Orient of today, when they express the thought that "all life is precious, therefore kill nothing "; because if you kill anything, it must of necessity react upon yourself, for all that exists on this planet is part of your body, part of the great God who rules this body, a part of your mind, and your mind a part of it. Again, all there is in the whole planetary system is a part of this one mind, this controller of all; and so on, from system to system, up to the Infinite itself, it takes all to constitute one grand unit.

Where, then, shall we look for the Highest? In the individual, the will is the supreme monarch: we cannot move a muscle without it so ordains. Has it form? No! we should define it rather as function. It has an organ, and that organ has form. Is it anything of form that causes me to move my arm? No! There is a centre of power — call it either if you choose. My hand moves quicker than thought: will has done it; the action produces thought. Has this thought form? Yes; thought has form called into existence by the mandate of the will formulated from the essence of the body. Each of you, my friends, are a thought-form of the solar mind, through which the God of this universe operates. A thought-form, an expression? Yes, a word of God. How truly John expressed this when he said, " in the beginning was the Logos," — the word; and the word was God, or power; and all things were made by it, or him: when the thought was formed, a world was born, and in that world was the essence of being that brought us here. You and I stand, a thought of that Infinite. Is that all? If we find that all that we call space is filled and intertilled with that which we call God, then what? We do not weaken our conception of God, but we are inevitably brought back to our Hebraic Bible, which states that God is everywhere present, and knows the heart and thoughts of every living soul. Yes; he knows! he thinks! If this were not so, how could you think and know? From whence did you receive the higher attributes that we call love? We love our wives and our children, and are willing to labor to uphold and maintain those dear ones. We derived these attributes from the fountain of all good, and yet we are a condition of matter; and although part of a great whole, are bound here and insphered within certain limits. But a mind has projected you into being, and that mind is everywhere. Man is a being of love, and there is nothing that can live without it: love is a magnet; it draws to, and embodies in itself, the object of its love. Without love, the grass could not grow, not a flower spring forth, not an animal organization could exist: no, it has formed all things; and therefore the wise man said, "God is love." Love is power.

When we refer to the ancient Cabala, and to the Hebraic Bible, we read that after a panoramic view of the whole order of creation, God said that all that he had made was very good; therefore we are right in attributing everything that is good to Love, for God is Love, and Love is power. There is nothing in nature but what is good; and when we call anything evil, it is because it opposes us. Now that mind of which you are the expression, of which everything that is, is an expression, by which all worlds were formed, is everywhere; and all the attributes possessed by human nature are everywhere. Take a thimble and hold it up; what does it contain? Atmospheric air. What more? Why, it contains enough of that infinite thought-potency to make a world, give it sufficient time. It contains so much of the infinite power that if you should breathe a desire, thought, or prayer to it, it would become a servant to your desire. Then pray always. Remember this: that this divine love, this divine thought, this divine wisdom, this infinite knowledge and infinite power, this will which holds in its right hand all these worlds, causing them to wheel around their centers, each in its appropriate orbit, — desires, yea, seeks, to serve you, but it cannot act other than in accordance with its nature; therefore conform to its nature, and it will be your servant. Remember, I repeat that this will which pervades everything is in you, and that it is Love; therefore strive to fulfill the commandments so forcibly expressed by the Nazarene, " Thou shalt love the Lord thy God with all thy heart, and with all thy soul, and with all thy mind . . . and thy neighbor as thyself."

Who is my neighbor? Every living thing, my fellow-man, even the reptile crawling at my feet, — all are a part of me, a part of my flesh, a part of my being; for I am a part of the grand man, and everything which is below me are but embryonic conditions of me, which will in time become man, taking my place. Then let us follow the commandment, and love God and our neighbor as it directs: then we shall find practical the idea of the Bagavad Gita, to arise and go up into some quiet, secluded spot, and think on me, even me, Om (the Sanscrit word for Omnipotent), and you shall find such meditation to be good for your soul.

Where shall we find the God of our ideal? In the quiet room, or lonely spot on the mountain top, or by the surging sea; wherever the mind can sit in calm meditation, and go out in this wonderful thought of the Infinite, tracing and following it wherever the imagination may lead, feeling certain that we cannot go astray; for it is God we seek, and God is infinite life and love and thought, infinite wisdom, power, and everything of which we can form any conception. When you know how to take hold upon yourself by the power of your own superior will, and then begin to think about that God, begin to imitate and try to be like him, and endeavor to bring your body and all its parts to the utmost perfection; begin to unfold, to think, to know, to will, to be, — then you commence to be like that Infinite; then the limits around you will begin to expand, the boundaries of the will will become wider and broader, and soon you will find that there are possibilities within you and within all that are so far beyond anything we have heretofore conceived, that we might imagine a man who possessed such power was the god of the universe.

יהוה

"I will be what I will to be."

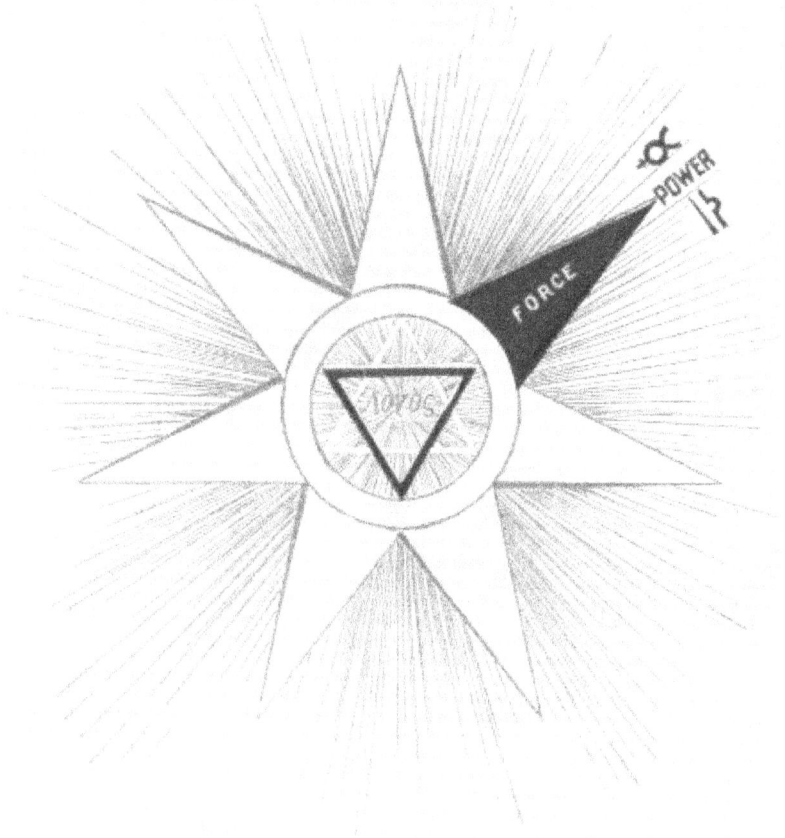

SECOND LECTURE. FORCE.

THE FIRST OF THE SEVEN CREATIVE PRINCIPLES.

In our last lecture we endeavored to bring before your minds a more comprehensive idea of God; to enable you to realize that God, the soul of the universe, is equally the soul of man. He is not a being, altogether unconditioned, beyond the bounds of time and space; nor is he a man, seated upon a high throne, in some far-away region, subject to human passions, and, like man, swayed by the force of circumstance. No, the Infinite Soul possesses and combines in itself all of the finer attributes of which we are enabled to form a conception. Everywhere that conscious being is present. Every thought, every word, is taken cognizance of by that superior intelligence. This fact, if regarded properly, would cause us to restrain many of our foolish thoughts and idle words, and would cause us to guard and control ourselves throughout life.

The object of considering, in these lectures, the seven creative principles, is to bring us into a mental condition where we shall cease to see evil as an absolute principle, and recognize the useful and good in everything. We learn that there is nothing in the universe, but what is necessary to the accomplishment of an ultimate purpose. When we come to realize this as a fact, or, as Paul expressed it, that "all things work together for good," we see that all things are working with unanimity and harmony, and for the purpose of forwarding a common object, viz., the building of a perfect man. What is most needed now is to look upon this world as a great factory, where men and all living things are engaged in the work of preparing our planet to become a paradise. When we get the thought clearly defined in our minds, that all Nature is working with us and for us, that we are parts of the Infinite Soul, and that, as parts thereof, we should overlook our father's workshop with the interest which sons should feel in caring for the factory of their father, then we shall be in harmony with Nature in all its forms.

Upon looking into Nature, we find that there are two great creative principles, the male and female, the divine and infinite father and mother.

The male and female principles pervade everything in Nature; the positive and negative, the centripetal and centrifugal. The two forces balance, and maintain an equilibrium. In consequence we are here. Were the positive principle to be released from the grasp of the negative, it would go out into space and be lost in the ether. It is the negative principle which gathers together, holds and concentrates, binds and preserves. Our planet, the Earth, has two poles on extremes, the north and the south; of these, the north represents the positive principle, the south the negative. The north has a greater area of cold than the south and belongs to the positive or masculine principle, while the south has less area of cold, but is more intense, and represents the negative or feminine principle. Thus the positive and negative are opposed to each other, and the currents of electricity passing from one to the other bind, enfold, and maintain all things in their appointed places. On looking into Nature we find that everything which grows is either positive or negative, male or female, that creation itself is carried on by these two factors.

When Moses went out of Egypt, as a keeper of Jethro's flock, his mind was stored with knowledge derived from the Egyptians. By reason of this knowledge he was enabled to develop his soul-powers to such an extent that he became capable of receiving and communicating with the Soul of the Universe. He became conscious of the existence of these two forces (the positive and negative), and of their great potency, without whose reciprocal action nothing which lives could have been brought into objective existence; and the two cherubs which he afterwards caused to be attached to the Ark of the Covenant, in conformity with the command given him upon Mount Sinai, were symbolical of these two forces.

Such knowledge and power as was possessed by the Hebrew Prophet may be attained by all of you if you but pursue the methods necessary for their attainment as diligently as did Moses.

In treating of the seven creative principles represented by this star, we will commence with the first, FORCE, which is negation. That which we call soul necessitated a change of condition before it could become that which we recognize as matter; therefore force, as one of the creative principles, must be brought to bear upon the universal soul or twelve electric oceans, to concrete matter as the basic substance of all objective forms.

The word " Logos " that appears in the centre of the diagram is in accordance with the thought expressed by John, who is accepted by all mystics as being a great cabalist. He began his gospel most wisely, when he said, "In the beginning was the Word ('The Logos'); the "Word was with God, and the Word was God . . . All things were made by him, and without him was not anything made that was made." Let us examine this more closely. If the word God meant power, we should read, " In the beginning was the Word, and the Word was with power, and the Word was power, and all things were made by it, and without it was not anything made that was made." This is evidently the true meaning of John.

In our consideration of God, the everywhere present and all-powerful Spirit of the universe, we think of it or him as we do of the power of thought. You form a thought preparatory to its expression. How is this done? The life-essences of your being are called together, concentrated in the brain, formulated in the mind, sent out by the will as a thing or entity.

16

Perhaps we had better pause here, and look a little deeper into this idea. We have said that a thought partakes of the essences of our own being. How do we know this? We know that when a man labors hard every day, that necessity obliges him to feed and sustain his body accordingly; if he is engaged in physical labor, the forces that are created through the food are absorbed by the body, and go no farther than physical energy, and are expended there. If the labor is mental, those forces are utilized by the mind. If a man is laboring very hard with his brain it is necessary for food to be furnished the body more abundant than when both body and mind were quiescent; this is evidence that the food we take into the body is for the purpose of supplying material from which this chemical laboratory of ours may transmute and bring into existence a subtle element which supplies and sustains the thought-formulating powers of the brain with its requisite material, and it is beyond question, as any thinking investigator may prove, and it has been proven thousands of times, that every word that we speak is formed of the essence of our being. To such an extent does this fact obtain that even the walls of the house in which we live partake enough of the essence of our being to enable sensitive persons, by taking a piece of paper from the walls, to draw from it, without having ever seen or even heard of its inmates, the same magnetism that was formulated and sent out by the brain and characterized by our essence; they will see us there, know our nature and character, and can describe us accurately; this, I say, has been proven over and again. Now, if this is a fact, it necessarily follows that every thought formed in our minds, and every word uttered by us to the mind or soul of others, appears like the thinker, partakes of every particle of our entire nature and being.

So, in the beginning was the Word. This infinite incomprehensible intelligence formed a thought, that was to create a world, and people it with man in its own image, and like unto itself. In the first chapter of Genesis, the twenty-sixth verse, we find these words: " Let us make man in our own image, after our likeness, and let them have dominion over the fish of the sea, and over the fowl of the air, and over the cattle, and over all the earth." The very central thought in the Hebraic Bible is expressed by this thought. The keynote of the whole subject is concentrated in the expression that the thought of the mind of the Infinite Spirit was to form a world and create beings like unto itself; and who, by possessing the powers and attributes of that spirit, should be enabled to control the fish of the sea, the fowl of the air, and all things in the earth; such is the thought that went into space with its dual activities.

We often say, " I conceived a thought." Yes, we conceive thought, through the agency of those dual principles ever active within us, and without which we cannot live. The two forces of the mind must tome together, or there is no power to think; every thought of ours is as much

17

our child, our offspring, as a child that is incarnate in the flesh, and comes into being by means of the same law, the same essence of being, without which essence we have nothing out of which to make a thought. Remember that the creative principles of Nature are the principles of generation, it underlies everything; every grain of sand upon which we tread, was once a living entity; we are constantly walking upon the ashes of the dead. Then the thought formed by the Infinite Soul and sent into Nature, was the Son of God. John spoke with great wisdom, when he said, "The word was made flesh and dwelt among us, and we saw His glory, as the glory of the only begotten of the Father." What did he mean? John was a philosopher, and he knew that he was speaking to people who were low down in the scale of understanding; he intended simply to convey the idea, that in the beginning the word of God formed a world; then the work of creation passed on through its successive stages of evolution, until finally, in the fullness of time, there stood forth one man in the world, who was able to demonstrate the fact that he had power over the fish of the sea, to say to them, "Bring the necessary tribute-money," and be obeyed by them, and to command both the animate and inanimate forces of Nature, and have their compliance to his mandates. He was the first man brought forth by the earth, to that people and in that age, who possessed such power. He was the expression of that power and thought, that went forth into space, and created worlds.

The word of God that was sent forth into space had in it principles of a triune nature; therefore we have illustrated upon the diagram, two triangles, representing the positive and negative, one the exact opposite and antithesis of the other. The triangle represents in its character, and has always done so from earliest history, first, the physical body as the base, with the spiritual and the soul or mental nature standing over; one side of the upper part of the triangle represents the soul, the opposite upper part represents spirit. These trinities, blended together, form the six-pointed star, and, in and through the workings of this double trinity, creation is what it is.

The father was always in the attribute of spirit; while to the mother has always been given the attribute of earth. Why? Because, the positive is centrifugal, goes out from the centre, scatters, ramifies, goes into space, ceases to be solidified, knows no bounds; while the negative reaches out and gathers in, lays hold of the positive and inspheres it, binds it within its own limits, and forms to itself the germ of being. It remains there until aided by the higher life-principle which we get from our solar ray, which gives it life; when it begins to draw additional strength, it begins to aspire, — yes, to pray. It reaches out, it gathers the sunbeams, it attracts the life-giving principle which strengthens its power to advance, for this sunbeam contains the positive and negative, the male and female principles, and the thought-forming principle; therefore within the material matrix is formed a thought, and that thought comes forth in its own image, let it be what it will, that of insect, reptile, animal, or bird. Thus thought breaks the shell of negation, and comes forth into light and life. Through the creative processes of nature the action of the magnetic principle gathers together the material essence, and that material essence, in its efforts to free itself, assumes function and some form of usefulness that was in the mind of the great thinker in the beginning, who planned their being and sent them forth to work his will; for will is the underlying power in all nature.

I want you, my thinking friends, who are wishing to unfold, and who are desirous of developing the higher powers, to think a great deal about the powers of the will. You cannot dwell too much upon this subject, for it will constantly expand and grow in your thought and life; it goes out into everything, and is found to be the active worker everywhere.

Force, then, is first, negative conservative magnetism, and is a principle of bondage or binding. It is a principle that, when carried into the realm of mind or matter, binds, restrains; and thus all men to-day are bound and held by woman. Every man is bound by her, — confined within the sphere of her limitations, out of which he cannot go without a struggle and effort of his own will; this, however, is not the voluntary action of her will, but is the magnetic potencies generated through her, and, as he cannot wholly escape limitations, neither can he advance save as she advances with him. Here then is laid the arena of combat, — of a struggle between the two great forces of creation which we now see active in domestic life, the positive and negative, between the effort of man to become spiritual and like his Creator, and the effort of the negative principle to hold and bind in the gestative sphere. The interior of woman is masculine. And it is incumbent on woman, at the present time, that she pause and think. Now this is contrary to her outward nature, which does not pertain to thought, but love; therefore she must think from the interior, the intuitive. She is magnetic, holding, binding, restraining the object of her love, to keep it within the limits of her own sphere; this is her outward nature; when she stops and thinks interiorly, reasonably and logically, she will find a place of higher usefulness where she can be free and become spirit, like the author of being, and thus advance with man.

In the seven creative principles we find there are seven struggles, as spoken of in the Apocalyptic vision; there are also seven steps that lead to the sacred temple, which was symbolized by Solomon's temple at Jerusalem. That which we are now considering is the first step of struggle and conquest, — the binding influence of the first of the creative principles. This principle of force must be subjugated by the higher will and intelligence; for, when we turn our attention toward ourselves, we find we are, in reality, spirit, though under the limitations of a physical body, which is binding, holding, and using our spiritual forces in the mere work of physical generation, in which the flesh begets flesh, and thus spirit goes on down the ages, inheriting bondage and imprisonment. If we would but recognize the fact that we are spirit, and, as such, in duty bound to hold control over these physical and generative forces, then would our inner and higher nature break the shell which inspheres and binds, and come into the light and freedom of the spirit.

Force, then, was the first principle of Nature, its magnetic focus attracted, concentrated, until atoms were gathered into an agglomerated mass. The astronomer points his telescope to the heavens and beholds nebulae. He sees these concentrated atoms in great quantities, without form. They are, as yet, without the second and third principles. Were they imbued with the second principle, discrimination, polarization, they would then begin to crystallize; and if they were endowed with the third principle, order, they would then begin to assume orderly structures. But they are not. They have simply been concentrated together by force. This force is operative everywhere. First, in the workings of Nature, atoms are concentrated, and by the power of positive and negative force, we have heat and cold, fire and water. As stated in our Bible, "In the beginning God created the heavens and the earth." In the Hebrew we find "Elohim" as the creator; in our translation it is rendered "God." Truly rendered, it would read, "Fire and water created the heavens and the earth; " fire the positive, water the negative, or heat and cold as the underlying cause. Through the operation of heat and cold atoms are formed and condensed as water; in these drops of water we see that there are worlds of living possibilities. The germs of being, when they were but molecules in the ether, had no objective form; but, as soon as they became a dense body of water, they absorbed enough of the solar ray to give life, they began to take form in this mass of water, and these forms fed upon the essences with which they were surrounded, and upon each other; and, as they generated their kind and increased, they died, and the solids that had thus been formed, commenced to deposit sediment at the bottom, and thus earth began. So we see that the world, at the beginning, was insphered and bound by this force of negation that gathered together the molecules or life-principles that formed atoms, and these, by the action of the two forces, were concentrated, and became water, which, in turn, brought forth living things; these living entities, having organs, generated their kind with great rapidity, and, as they expended the vitality that was within them by generating other organisms, they became ashes, and settled to their appointed centre of gravity, as controlled by the enveloping and binding magnetic and electric sphere.

If we should take a glass globe, fill it with water, put in sediment, and then begin to turn it slowly, we would find that, after a while, the sediment in the globe would form a hollow tube running from pole to pole, but if we had the globe so arranged that we could constantly change the axe of this rotation, instead of forming a hollow T tube, it would form a round sphere, wherein there would be water inside and water outside. The sphere would be larger or smaller, according to the rapidity with which we turned the globe. This solves, to my mind, the mystery of how this earth was formed, and that it is, undoubtedly, a hollow globe, having water at the centre as well as water outside. Probably, however, that through ages of continued compression there may have been enough heat to decompose the water and leave only a heated mass of gases, hydrogen, and oxygen.

As the water brought forth its kind, and they died, their ashes formed solids, though the globe had probably not then begun to revolve; for, very likely, before this motion began, it was like the nebula that had no revolution until the solids have formed sufficiently to settle to their centre of gravity, where, by compression, and by the principle of negation which concentrates and binds, and by virtue of which compression of chemical elements, chemical change took place, and by those changes there were electric forces sent out from pole to pole, both positive and negative. These again, by contact, created new currents, and from the heat caused by compression, expansion undoubtedly took place, of which we find evidences all over the earth, such as volcanic mountains and other upheavals, which indicate the force generated by compression and chemical action. We have also to notice that there is a magnetic current flowing up and down as well as north and south, from pole to pole. This can be proved by taking an iron bar, — the ordinary stove-poker will suffice for the experiment, — stand it upright against a chair, then take a magnetic needle and place it against the bottom of the poker, and you will find that the south pole of the needle will turn to the poker, showing that the lower end is negative; move the needle up the poker, and you will find that as it passes the middle it will turn around, and the north pole of the needle will point to the poker. This shows that there is sufficient current, up and down, to polarize an iron bar in from five to fifteen minutes' time.

This up-and-down current is the emanation of decomposing mineral substance, and is the emblem or element of decomposition and death. This, to our eyes, is darkness and death, because it is the opposite of light and life. Being the opposite of the current that emanates from the sun, therefore, we find it flowing towards the sun, to which it holds a negative relation. On the contrary, the rays of the sun are positive, and impart force, motion, life. Let us consider a globe, — a planet exposed to its rays. It becomes magnetic by induction, and gets its polarity or axis north and south; but, in addition, there is an electric energy which results from the action of light; this again arranges itself according to electric laws, and one side of the globe becomes positive, and is repelled from the sun, while the other, being negative, is attracted, and thus revolution on its axis is established. To further illustrate, let us imagine this watch to be a ball, and that above is the sun. The side toward the sun gets light and heat; we turn it a little, and the dark, cold portion is presented; the sun's rays strike upon the cold portion, and there is mutual attraction; but where it is light and hot, having absorbed its equivalent and become like the sun, it is repelled, as can be readily demonstrated by simple electrical experiments. Therefore, we realize that the earth must continue to revolve, in the ratio of the electric energy that is brought to bear upon it, and we have no reasons to apprehend a diminution of the supply.

Light is an element, just as much as water; and you may be aware that watch-dials and other articles are now being made, which have the capacity of absorbing enough of this element, during the day, to enable one to see the time, at night, without the aid of other light. So is darkness an element, but it pertains to death and decomposition; and, therefore, the human mind quite naturally associates black, as the symbol of death and grief. We find man, as a rule, acts wiser than he is aware, as intuition leads him to do many things with greater perfection than he comprehends. If we watch the action of children, we will find the same thing is true, and that they often manifest an instructive method and that their actions are in conformity with a reason beyond their comprehension; and this is so because there is an infinite soul that animates and guides their being.

Thus we see that there is an active, attractive, and enveloping principle in nature that set this earth in motion, and, when motion commenced, it begun to take form. Life and creation commenced in the water, and went steadily forward. Sediment deposited, chemical action took place, and upheaval followed upheaval, and when there was a sufficient amount of solid matter above the water, vegetation began to form. Of necessity I have been obliged to encroach upon the work of the other principles, for there can be no progressive formation without the operation of the principles of order and discrimination, and these principles are present, and, to a certain extent, active, even hi the molecules and atoms before they become water.

In summing up this lecture we desire not only to give you the principles of the subject, but to impress you with their direct bearing and use to-day; yet it is well to say that, during this course of lectures, there may be some points of philosophy that may not be clear to you, and you may not be able to understand all their practical bearings and use; but you must keep in mind that there are two objects to be attained, as expressed in the earlier portion of the lecture, viz., to bring your mind to the comprehension of the fact that all creation is working together for your ultimate good, that you may be brought into harmony with nature in its objective and higher degrees, and those of you reading the subsequent lectures to the society will have the benefit of more direct and practical instruction. Again, as we advance, methods of attainments will be given, higher degrees unfolded by which you can gain control over yourselves and the forces of nature, whereby you may become sons and masters, instead of servants. Therefore, as we proceed, you will find that these thoughts are but stepping-stones to that which lies beyond, " within the veil, " and which must, of necessity, for the present, to some degree at least, seem mere matter of theory; but, later on, to those of you who follow out and make the required attainments, they will become matters of realized fact, having served as a bridge enabling you to pass over the chasm and enter the new world of thought and power.

יהיה

"*I will be what I will to be.*"

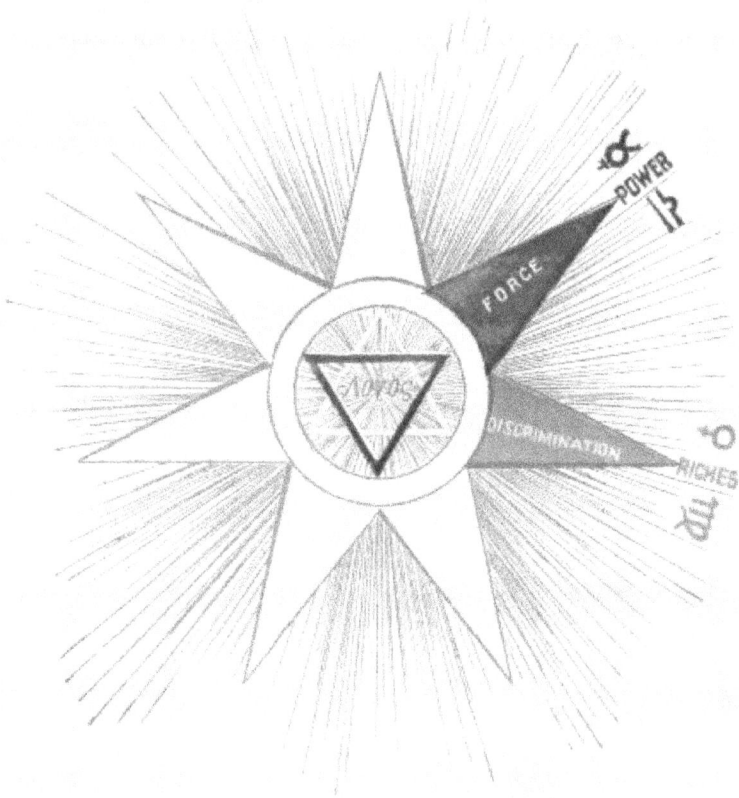

THIRD LECTURE. DISCRIMINATION.

THE SECOND OF THE SEVEN CREATIVE PRINCIPLES.

In our last lecture we considered the subject of world building, under the leadership of the first principle of the seven creatives, — Force. We called your attention to the fact that this force, being negative, called into existence a sphere, not by itself alone; for it is impossible for us to consider these seven principles, in their operation in the world, entirely separate one from another, as they work together, and no one of them can work entirely independent of the other. They are united together in their action, as literally in all their workings, as they are in the diagram of the star that represents them. Therefore, all through the consideration of these principles we are forced to take each of the seven as a head, controller, and subjugator, we may say, of the other principles, that are acting jointly with it.

These seven principles are the foundation and means by which the multifarious conditions that we see in the world arise into objective existence; and, as the mind scans the vast world-radius and workings of these principles in their successive stages, we are lost, and feel like turning away as from a task beyond the possibility of human intelligence; but, having before us a diagram which is the formula that expresses these principles, we are enabled to take up each, and trace them in their creative workings.

In the operation of this second principle, discrimination, which is the subject for consideration in this lecture, we observe that it is, in itself, first, the manifestation of the polarizing principle. "We are told that even atoms have polarity, and that polarity gives them the nature of attraction and repulsion, which is the manifest action of discrimination. This polarization will be seen in its first phase of operation by taking two needles, polarize them with a magnet, and then lay the positive pole of one to the positive pole of the other, on a piece of paper, and they will immediately fly apart; reverse them, turning the negative pole of one to the positive pole of the other, and they will come together. Here is the first manifestation of the law of discrimination, — a principle in nature that discriminates as to the relation of atom to atom. This principle is not only found in the atom, but it is the prime factor in all formation; but, of course, without the third principle united with it, it would only build together the atoms of matter, not in the form of molecules, or even in the form of vegetation, but it would simply build together in a straight line, which line might continue on and on eternally. We know that we can take a bar-magnet, cut it in two as many times as we please, and every piece will still be a magnet, having positive and negative poles which would come together just as it was cut apart, in the same direction, one to the other. That is to say, none of the pieces could be turned around and put back in place and adhere; but if the pieces were all kept in the same direction, and then put together they would cohere by the power of the magnetism that was within them; but take the pieces and turn them about hither and thither, and then put them together; some of them would be repelled, and some would fly together. This law of discrimination is found operative at the very base of material formation. It would be unwise in us, at this time, to attempt to trace this law further in the building processes of nature, because, in so doing, we should have to intrude upon our next lesson; therefore we will endeavor, in this lecture, to regard it in its more fully developed phase, where it will be useful to us; and its growing process and building powers will be considered under the law of order, in the lecture on the third principle.

We find, in our relations to each other, that the same principle of discrimination is operative between man and man, also between beasts, birds, insects, and with everything that has life; it is observed that discrimination is manifested in a natural attraction and natural repulsion. These principles of attraction and repulsion in matter are but the same conditions or the same principles that we see operative in the relations of mind. As from mind all things came, into mind all things return; therefore we can logically and reasonably trace this action in animate nature, as we call it, from the inanimate and gross element to the thought and will of man, and find that our thoughts, feelings, and emotions are controlled by exactly the same principles.

This principle of discrimination is the principle that keeps in purity all things that are. Were it not for this principle we would have nothing distinct. There would be no gold, silver, iron, vegetable or animal formations; there would be nothing but a formless mass brought together with all qualities intermixed. You must readily see that, without this principle of discrimination, there could be nothing but chaos. This principle is active in everything that is, whether it has or has not animate life. This is the cause of our pronouncing so many things in the lower order of nature as being bad, and accounts for a feeling of antagonism; for instance, we want to kill snakes, lizards, and all reptiles; in fact, there is a natural repulsion to all things below us, otherwise we should absorb their qualities and descend to their level.

Many who have begun to think and observe these laws of mind have concluded, because of this strong repulsion and attraction, that those persons that they were repelled from must, of necessity, be evil; that there must be something about them that was bad, or else they would not be so repelled by their presence. The ignorance of the law of discrimination leads them to this conclusion; but we must not be too hasty, but should remember that while such persons may be evil to them, and doubtless are, that they are no more evil in the aggregate than they themselves.

Perchance they may be superior persons in every way, and yet this repulsion be felt; in fact, there are few persons in the ordinary walks of life, who, if they should meet a man possessed of the attainments of some of the grand masters that we read of in the works of antiquity, but what, as soon as they should come into their presence, would feel a repulsion, and shrink away from them. We might very readily imagine that the person was evil, and do often so imagine. When people on the present plane of life find a man or woman that is really, in all their characteristics, superior to themselves, they do not understand them, and feel repelled. They see that such persons are self-possessed, and at once imagine evil concerning them; multifarious evil conjectures arise in their minds, until, perchance, it may even seem proper to do them violence, or subject them to the law for imprisonment. The Nazarene implied this when he said, "Ye are not of this world; if you were of this world, the world would love its own; but ye are not, therefore the world hates you." Therefore, when we come to consider this law of discrimination, we find that, often we meet persons that at first sight hate us, that are possibly even malignant, and seek every opportunity to bring us into condemnation, and to provoke us to do something that will put us in their power; why do they do it? Is it because they are vicious and bad? Not at all. It is because they are themselves on a low plane of life; they love that plane of life, and, as soon as one with a higher nature comes into their atmosphere, they feel that there is something in them that is breaking up and interfering with their plans of life, which is, in a measure, true, and they at once begin to antagonize them, and to seek for some grounds of condemnation; and we know how prolific the imagination is when people get the idea that there is something bad in another, how easy it is to distort some of the best acts of life, and transform them into appearance of a desperate character. We must expect these things in life, because of the potent factors in the workings of creation. This is one of the causes (there are many others however) that induced all the ancients, who made great attainments in the mastery over self and in controlling the power of the elements, to seek isolation from the world; they retired into the wilderness, into caves where they could be separated from their fellows, where they could be free from those antagonisms from which they would otherwise have to suffer, and this was well on their part; but we believe that the conditions are not so adverse to-day.

We have reasons now to believe that there are a great many people, who have become so fully unfolded in their interior or higher nature, that they are ready and anxious to let go of this lower nature, — this lower condition of life, — and step upon a higher plane of being. This principle has developed in them a discrimination between right and wrong, between error and truth, between the descending currents of involution, and the ascending currents of evolution, to which all things are subject. And ever in our physical bodies these two currents, of necessity, continue their action, and will so do whilst we remain in the flesh. In fact, I doubt there ever coming a time, in all the stages of progress that we may make in the ages to come, that these two currents will not be active in our bodies.

The descending currents of involution are by virtue of prayer. What is prayer? The very act in itself, calls out, as a prime factor, the law of discrimination; You desire. Desire what? You discriminate even in your desire. You desire something, not everything. You are, then, like the needle that points to the pole. You at once concentrate all your thoughts, all your desire, on whatever object you determine. If you desire knowledge of the cause-world, you begin by reaching out to the great centre of cause. You formulate an idea of what that centre is, what its nature is, what its qualities are, and, after you have formulated the idea of the nature and qualities of that first great cause, you then centre or polarize the magnets of your desire upon that central source. You desire to have the knowledge of that infinite mind. That desire then becomes a powerful magnet, which reaches out into the spheres above, and lays hold upon the substance of its desire, and brings it down and incorporates it into your being; it is aspiration that goes out and gathers the substance that it needs and incorporates it into the very centre of being. It is the law known and acted upon by the Sages.

It is said in " Yoga Philosophy " that if we concentrate our mind on the north polar star, we obtain knowledge of Astronomy; on the sun, Spiritual Wisdom; on the moon, knowledge of Earth; if on the palm of the hand, knowledge of future events, etc.

The response does not come into the head first, neither into the reason, but into the centre of the love-nature; for Love is the magnet, and, unless we cultivate the law of love, we shall never acquire the magnetic power that will enable us to reach out and gather the things we need. Love is the only power in the world. In our previous discourse upon the first of the seven principles (Force), we told you that it was negative, feminine in its nature; and we now tell you that the feminine or the nature of the female is, externally, love; while the interior of man is negative, feminine in its character, and thus love in its operation. Love, then, without the activity of this principle of discrimination, would become a force that would gather around it all kinds of useless elements, and make up a heterogeneous mass of confused ideals. It would, in practice, amount to evil obstructions; but, loving, we must have a definite idea of what we love. Here is where our Mother Church has made a great mistake. It has taught us that we are to love every person; love your enemies, love the wicked as well as good, but we must discriminate in our love between loving the man, the person and the divine principle that animates him. We know that all life is good; that this animating principle, wherever it is found, let it be in man, in your brother, your loved companion, or in the most loathsome serpent that is creeping in the swamps, that life is good; it is a part of the infinite, and must, of necessity, be good. It is the animating principle. We call it by a variety of names, but it is the spirit that animates all being. Now, we discriminate in our love. We love what? The good! God is good! God is the only good! — the only good that maintains, supports, and sustains all things. But now we are speaking of absolute good.

There is absolute good, which is spirit; there is relative good, which is a condition of usefulness. It is necessary for us here to make a fine point of discrimination. Anything that is useful to assist one in accomplishing their object is regarded as good; but anything that hinders or obstructs one's plan or design is considered evil. This, however, is but relative good and relative evil. In the broad sense there is no such thing as absolute evil, but there is such a thing as absolute good.

Let us consider this principle of discrimination in its relation to prayer, which is the love-principle turned towards one's highest ideal of God, or good, with the desire to receive that we stand in need of; we thus draw down and incorporate in ourselves the substance of things desired. Now, as to the result. At first it enters the interior of our being, the love-nature. It takes form in the essences of our life, is carried up to the brain, formulated into thought by the power of reason, and thus the inspiration becomes to us a revelation. For then that which we have inspired from the higher spheres through the action and aspiration of our love, entering into our life, forms itself into reason, and, being a thought-form, stands out before us in its image, in the exact form of the principle of which it is the expression. Now, this is inspiration, and revelation is its consequent result. The receiving is the inspiration, the formation in the intellect is the revelation, and it is thus that we gather to ourselves something that we did not possess before, something higher, something grander than we had. That which we before loved and clung to we now hate because we have no more use for it. In its relation to this higher and grander it becomes evil; and, because of discrimination, we repel it from us, we spurn it, we say it is error, we must break that habit; if persevered in it will bring inconvenience, disease, and suffering.

The new revelation that has been made to our mind, by the law of discrimination says: "Repel! " From this state comes the mental condition that promotes the work of evolution. The incoming of a higher condition produces a spontaneous unfoldment of mind. Now, what is it that is involved in our nature? It is the thought-crystallization of former expressions; and, when we repel and throw them off, they go down into a lower plane where they are drawn in, insphered and become a part of the lower elements, and make room for the new and higher conditions in ourselves. It is well known that vegetation feeds on that which human life throws off. And the animal world also feeds mentally from the thought-potency that the human mind exhales; so that these very principles that are to-day a part of our soul-life, and which would otherwise go with us into another stage of being, may be, and should be, thrown off, and go down into the lower stages of being. In other words the lower stages of existence aspire towards us. They seek and reach up to us as we do to that which is above, — to God. They feed from the overflow of our nature as we from the infinite essence. That is the law of involution; the flowing down of the surplus elements, through us, to the very lowest stages of being. They are, when once disintegrated, scattered as it wore, torn to pieces, and every part scattered to its place. The law of discrimination, it is thus perceived, works most diligently in nature. As these elements descend indiscriminately, this principle of discrimination causes each to take just what part it needs, and to repel all beside, exactly as does the little seed in its process of germination and growth. We, perchance, take two seeds, one whose nature is bitter, the other sweet, make a hole in the ground, drop those two tiny seeds into it; they lie side by side, the same moisture softens and expands, the same sunlight warms them, they germinate, they grow up side by side. Their stalks at once begin to draw away from each other, and we can scarcely find two such seeds but what, when their stalks come up through the ground, would be some distance apart, as far apart as they can well got, for they are repelled each by the other. Their roots are all mingled together, drawing their sustenance from the same earth and the same sun; one repels all the bitter elements, and attracts all the sweet; the other attracts all the bitter and repels all the sweet. They grow up together, and each maintains its own nature, regardless of the fact that they were germinated side by side, regardless of the fact that their roots were interwoven and they are drawing their sustenance from the same fountain in every particular.

So this principle of discrimination has relation to the law of involution, and even the effete elements that are thrown out from our bodies, even the thought-potencies, which are elements, as I have shown you previously, are carried down to the lower plane of being, where each thing in its order attracts parts of it, takes it up, scatters it, builds new organisms, and, as these new organisms are built, they begin the work of aspiration, which is the factor in evolution. Observe the plant come out of the ground; two little leaves; then, right out from the centre of these two, comes another, and thus the plant grows from the interior. Finally, the first two leaves die and fall back to the earth to nourish other plants. They grow and unfold from the centre; from the innermost they grow out and become the outermost, and then in turn they fall off, and out from the innermost again come others. Such is the expression of our life, if we are as active and as diligent, intellectually and spiritually, as the vegetable kingdom below us, and we certainly should be.

The mind that is not active, desiring knowledge, desiring wisdom and understanding, expanding to its uttermost power to obtain knowledge, to obtain understanding of all that is around it, is not doing as well as the humble growing plant.

All life is growing by force of circumstances, and these aspiring, and these descending elements become to us an incentive to reach out, to aspire to something better and better, therefore, from this interior consciousness, we are constantly discriminating between elements and conditions that we have already attained, that have served their purpose, and those which we are still reaching out for and desiring to secure. Then let us learn this lesson from the plant, never to stop growing, so long as life and opportunity remains. What we know to-day should not satisfy us to-morrow.

I can say for myself that there is no pleasure, worthy of the name of pleasure, that is obtainable through any other means than through the procuring of knowledge.

We talk about pleasurable sensations; if we discriminate accurately we will discover that many sensations are at the expense of our life, and not in reality pleasure, but rather a form of pain. It is only the ideal that gives pleasure. When we are imbued with a knowledge of the cause-world, and begin to reach out and inspire from that great fountain of knowledge, our appetite is spoiled for that which the world calls pleasure, — the pleasure of the senses; we then find no true pleasure save in thinking the thoughts of the Infinite.

The thoughts of the Infinite express themselves in nature in the workings of the seven creative principles, first, in their primitives, and fully in their ultimates. We find that the angel, in his revelation to John, 5, 12; named the ultimates of the seven creative principles in the following language. Worthy is the Lamb that was slain to receive 1st, Power; 2d, Riches; 3d, Wisdom; 4th, Strength; 5th, Honor; 6th, Glory; 7th, Blessing. " These thoughts of God are the true Riches.

We find that all sensations in the incidents of life, that which the world calls pleasure, is rather the exhaust, the wasting of the life-element. Whilst this is going on there is sensation, and we imagine it is pleasure; whereas, if we discriminate accurately and carefully, we find it is pain. It is the working of death and destruction; but, when we are carrying this life-force up to the higher stage of transmutation, by virtue of conquering the lower passions, conquering all waste in the line of sensations and the generative energies, we turn it up to the brain and mature it there, forming thoughts and sending them forth to do our will, through which means life is matured more perfectly, and our senses are made finer, the workings of these senses become so harmonious that they are to us like the most delightful music, like the music of the spheres. We will find our higher thoughts are extremely pleasurable, when in accord with this law of inspiration that is ever active in us; that is the power of our being; that gave us birth; whose power, as we have shown you, is that love that reaches out and lays hold on the life of the infinite and perfect Soul, drawing it down into the centre of our being, where it fills our whole nature, thrilling it and animating: it from centre to circumference. And, when it is called up to the brain, oh, what pictures it makes in our intellect! what thoughts of a perfect being! Think of it, the thoughts of the perfect thinker! Why perfect? Because the law of discrimination has done its perfect work! Every line of demarcation has been distinctly made; all unfit elements have been eliminated, it has rejected all that was unfit and impure, and has selected the purest and finest of all things in nature; therefore it is filled with the true riches, the life of the Infinite Soul.

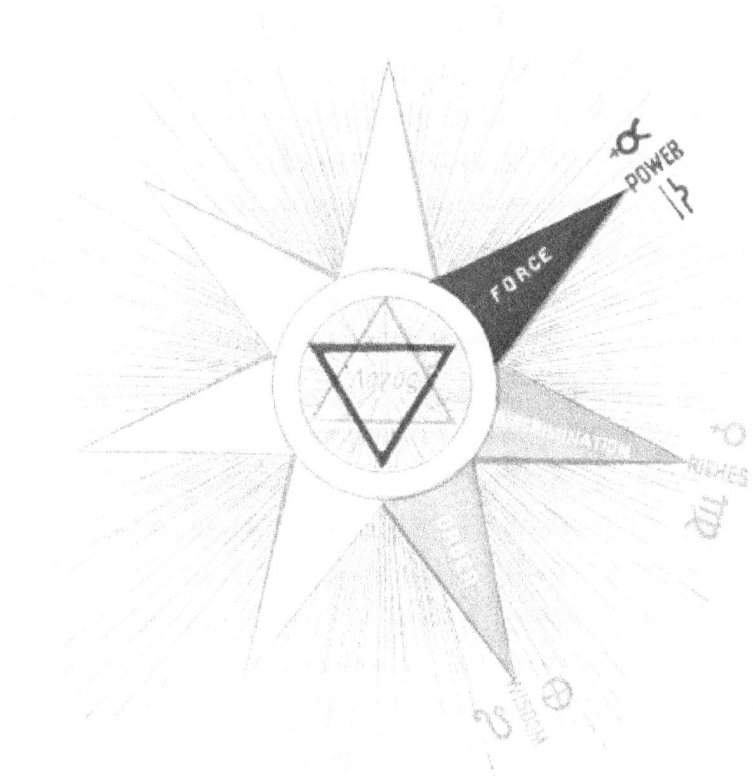

FOURTH LECTURE. ORDER.

THE THIRD OF THE CREATIVE PRINCIPLES.

These thoughts on order, the third principle of creation, lead us to consider its first manifestation in nature. Having laid down a foundation-principle in the first lecture, on "The Idea of God," we are now ready to present a more complete understanding of this third principle in its unity with the other two. Now, this third principle, united with the two previous, brings us to manifest organization. In its first phase the atom is polarized and endowed with order, and, by virtue of their innate endowments, form into orderly structures by the action of cold and heat.

How many times have I stood, in my childhood, also in manhood, and looked upon the pictures drawn by the Divine Artist, as the frost gathered and pictured upon the window-pane beautiful swamp-scenes, where the forms of vegetation in great variety were represented. Again have I paused as I walked along the streets, after a rain followed by freezing, where the water, by virtue of the cold, had concentrated and congealed, and stood out upon the pavement in the form of a beautiful vine or a lovely tree, thus imaging the growth of vegetation. And, as I looked upon these scenes, my thoughts at once went back to the mind that endowed matter with this potential, orderly energy.

Jesus, the Nazarene, expressed but little more when he said, "As the Father hath life in himself, so hath he given to the Son to have life in himself." And as the Father and author of all being has life, order, mind-power, and intellect in himself, so all that emanates from that infinite mind has the same attributes innate in themselves; therefore, as we walk through this grand old earth of ours, and see the beauteous structures created by this in-dwelling divine mind, how can we help but worship. But, as we see the frost gathering upon the window-pane, or upon the flag-stone, or congealed in the tumbler or in the creek, those beautiful forms have but three principles combined; therefore, these crystals are not substantial, but as soon as the fourth principle is added to them, the principle of cohesion, which in itself is heat, it at once dissipates them; it becomes a destroyer; it tears down and prepares them to come up in vegetable life, where they can be further matured.

These two forces, the positive and the negative, cold and heat, are the formative agents of nature; and, wherever they meet and produce these sub or transient formations, they leave the essences of such endowed with a principle of life that causes vegetation to spring up and life to be manifested in all its various forms in nature. These principles, of which order is the third, are active in the formation of all crystallization, and we find them

34

manifest in minerals, where the different chemicals combine, and crystallization takes place; and in each case they assume a definite form, according to quality. Every crystal that is possessed of perfect essence — that is, where the law of discrimination has its full force — will take a regular shape. Probably all of you have seen those beautiful crystallizations brought from the West and elsewhere, where they have formed the octagon, and the different angles and ovals, and all the various shapes, as accurately as if they had been made by some artisan, and had been formed for an express use. We cannot but admire and wonder when we look into nature, and see in it these beautiful expressions of the infinite mechanic that are so like the effort of the human hand and brain.

As we consider the law of order, it leads us further into the realm of vegetable life, where we see atoms gathering together, taking shape, coming forth in the form of whatever quality they possess; and here we see the trinity of principles. First, the solids are concentrated by force; by the maternal or mother-principle the magnet thought draws together and inspheres and binds; then comes the second principle, discrimination, giving it polarization, when it begins to resist the concentrative power; and then comes in the master-workman, order, and calls everything into its place. Discrimination came, and said, " This atom must not be gathered up by this, and this must not be gathered up by that "; then order, says, " This belongs here, the other belongs there"; and so goes on the work of both, so that, two seeds of a different nature being planted side by side, the same water will nourish them, the same soil will supply their common needs; but each of these, by virtue of their discriminative power, will reject certain chemical elements, and, by order of the master-workman, they take others, carry them to their destination, and deposit them in their place, the one chosen by the great architect of nature. Should there be something that would interrupt the workings of the law of order in matter, we would see at once that there was malformation in plants, trees, and animal life, such as abnormal growths, knots on plants and trees; also, false growth in animal bodies. These are the workings of the three principles: the first collects the elements; the second selects the qualities; and the third takes them and places them where they belong. Can there be found a principle in mechanics working together with greater harmony, with greater accuracy, than these principles work, in their chemical selections, and in their orderly structure building? I think not.

We cannot but admire and wonder when we look into this process, and see a mind at work there whose capacity so far surpasses the human intellect. This law of order, united with the other principles, gives every plant, every vegetable, and every animal their distinct form, by virtue of the quality of the germ-life coming from its parental source. That germ-life has been organized with power to gather around it like elements, to mature principles of which it was the expression, and it always carries it out to the letter of the law, making no mistakes; so we are in the habit of looking into each other's faces, and saying, "You look like your mother," and "you look like your father," and so on. Again, we look into each other's faces, and we read there the nature of the person. "We say that person has something good; that person is disposed to live in this or that way. How do we know? We know only because this divine architect has done his work perfectly. He has made no mistake; he has expressed his thought in perfect language. Not only has he done this so that we may read character from physiognomy or phrenology of mankind, but this principle of reading character from the language of form, was the first principle of thought. As animals came into being on this planet and began to devour one the other, self-protection became the one thought most necessary; and in the work of self-protection there came fear, and they at once began to take cognizance, and to look at and judge of the objects that were approaching them, whether they should fear them or not.

Thus, animals began to recognize the image of a thing before they did the nature of it; this must, of necessity, be the first starting-point, — that of judging from physiognomy, as we call it. "We go into the woods, and the wild beasts know each other. Some will feed together because they realize that they do not antagonize each other, and, as soon as an antagonistic beast comes along, they flee for their lives. How do they know? Here, again, the language of form stands out, and they know from the image what is combined and embodied in the form.

They know, at least, this, that it is a form of antagonism and destruction to them. Thus, the faculty of mind in man to-day, that enables him to judge of things and qualities by form, is the most perfectly developed faculty in the human brain; and this should be the one that we utilize to the greatest advantage. In my thought and study, years past, I saw that every line upon the face spoke a language; and every mark that comes there, without injury, tells a story; it speaks of some in-working principle. Yes, every line upon the hand is a hieroglyphic that tells of one's minute character; even the formation of the nails on the fingers, the shape of the hand, every minute particle of the man, reveals the character therein expressed. Think of such a mechanism! Think of a mind that is capable of causing nature to come together so perfectly in accordance with the language of its own inner being! This lesson is ever before us, we see it on every side; and the more we think upon it, the more will we realize its truth.

We so into the woods, and, whilst anions the trees, we find, springing up, a little leaf. We do not know what it is; to us it is mute. We present it to a botanist, who makes a story of plant-life; he observes its color, its outline, the lines upon it, the thickness, the little fibers, — all its minutiae unite together to tell him the history of the plant to which it belongs. Then, at once, he becomes a prophet, a fortune-teller, and tells you that if you see that shrub in the fall, when it is fully matured, you will find on it berries of such and such qualities, and that it possesses such and such chemical properties, etc. lie can tell you everything about it, just from one leaf. Think what an orderly workman Nature is! We do not find thistle-leaves on apple-trees, nor cabbage-leaves growing on potato-plants.

We do not sufficiently consider the wonderful wisdom that is working under this divine order to cause the chemistry of this world; the molecules fly through the atmosphere, seemingly without any government; the wind sweeps hither and thither, everything apparently going by chance, all being hurled together here and there; but stop! In it all is that wonderful mind — that wonderful mechanic — that, no matter how it is hurled together and mixed up by the upheaval of forces, and cyclones of wind and storm or rain, it never makes any mistakes, but always gets everything in its right place. Now, the human mind has the most perfect development in that function, more so than in any other of its nature. That function is the one that has built our railroads; that has made up our mechanical interests; that has actuated the workingman, as he hewed and chopped away at the great oaks that once covered this land, who squared and built them into the crude houses, — the law of order in the brain of that mechanic enabled him to rear the structure. But, look again; he conceives a way of obviating much of this hard labor. He goes to work and invents machinery; he carries this divine order that he sees everywhere working in nature into a mechanical device to do his work, to save his strength, to relieve his muscles.

On and on we have gone, until now the more subtle forces of nature are under our control. By bringing into orderly forms certain mechanical appliances we control the lightning, bring it down, and make it our errand-boy to carry the messages, not only from house to house, and from one city to another, but through the very depths of the great ocean, from shore to shore. This is the law of order, as it is working in the human mind. It imitates nature, and observes cause and effect, how one thing acts upon another, produces combinations like the machinery of a watch, or other machinery where speed of movement is required, and where the cogs, intercepting each the other, each wheel must have definite proportion to the other. For, if they lessen the one and increase the other, they increase the speed; herein the human brain begins to imitate the divine architect. But this imitation goes but a short distance. It simply takes the material that has been created by that divine power, and forms the structure for us by physical or mechanical effort; but there is a step beyond this, — that is, if we carry out the imitation of that divine mind, — that is, the workman in nature. We do not see a man-god coming down and, by his hand, taking these atoms and putting them in their place, and giving them form as a child would build cob houses; but we perceive a mind-power that is enabled to send forth thought, to endow nature with that tendency to cause a world to build itself, and not only to cause a world to be built, but regulated and controlled in all the minutiae of structure. After we have scanned all the visible objects on the planet earth, we have taken only the first step toward beholding all that there is. We take the magnifying lens and a single drop of water, and discover there is a little world within itself, all tilled with active, organized life. This great mechanic has gone down into minutiae, where it takes a lens magnifying seven, eight, and ten thousand times in order that our eyes can discern what is going on, and yet this wonderful mechanic has gone to work there, has made a structure that is perfect; yes, and sometimes, as we scan those beautiful little things, we think that nature has been partial to them, because of the beauty, agility, activity, and vivacity that they manifest. Now, if we turn from this small world and direct the telescope to the heavens, there again we find the architect and mechanic at work. All is order, perfect order, perfect harmony. There we find other worlds, hundreds of times larger than our own, indications of far greater complications in their workings; suns millions of times larger than our world, and these all flying through space with lightning speed; suns and systems of worlds moving around their centers. To think of this intelligently, to realize it, we stand in awe at such a presence, — a presence that is even under our feet. As we stand upon the solid earth, that divine principle is changing the grains of sand upon which we rest, taking of their qualities; and, notwithstanding we are pressing upon them, they are actually changing and being built into other forms.

We are told, in the Hebrew Bible, that the declared purpose of God was " Let us make man in our own image and like us; and let him have dominion over the fish of the sea and the fowl of the air, and over all the earth." That is very sweeping. — " all the earth;" and such words from a mind that is so discriminative, so orderly! What a declaration from such a source, that these microscopic objects, those mighty suns and worlds, every objective thing, with their governing law and creative engines, — man to have dominion over all this! "What kind of man would this necessitate? How many, many millions of cycles must pass, ere such will be manifested on this planet?

But let us consider this subject from another point of view: the habit we have formed of recognizing friends, of determining qualities in persons, in animals, in things in general. This habit we find so established that it goes on imaging, even in our sleep, so that, if we dream, the act of dreaming is to see images. What is a dream? Perhaps we are lying in our beds, resting quietly; but, whilst we dream, we see ourselves somewhere, perhaps in danger, struggling with antagonistic forces, their images appearing to us, perchance as wild beasts. How real it all seems to us for the time; and in the struggle, perhaps, we wake up, come back to our normal consciousness to find that it was not real. What has caused it? The physician will tell us there was a derangement in the digestive forces; there sometimes is; we find that, if we have taken something into the stomach that has chemically fermented and produced gases foreign to our nature, these elements or gases press upon the brain. The brain is thus forced to act whilst the body sleeps, and it images forth the antagonistic essences that are generated in the body; and, if it were possible for one to be so fine a chemist as to be able to trace the workings of this law of order to the very animals that you saw in your dream, you would find there was some bond of relatedness and chemical cause for the objects imaged, that the chemical nature of the beast seen was like that produced in the stomach through the derangement. This is where the law of order is interrupted in the digestive function, which works faithfully on the brain. When we have become the wonderful chemists that we shall be some time, we will then know just exactly what chemical properties produce each given result upon the mind as well as upon the physical body, so that we will be enabled to extract the thought-essence that produced the plant, and then the contact with the human nerve will produce like thought-essence and imaged likeness.

I told you there are but seven creative principles in all nature. No matter where you go, these, in their different combinations, produce all the qualities that there are. But, whilst these seven are creative principles, they are not qualities of things; for qualities of things are wholly related to conditions in the stages of transmutation. Transmutation goes to a higher degree in some natures than in others. The chemistry of the body is more perfect in some organisms than in others, and, therefore, it does finer work; so the difference in quality that we find in matter is owing to the stage of change or unfoldment.

"We find these elements and chemicals in the sunray and in the atmosphere above us. As the worlds are changing in their position, the solar fluid is being changed and altered systematically. According to this definite mechanical law there are constantly changing thought-potencies being imparted to the world; and, as these changing thought-potencies are received, it affects all vegetation and animal life. When the human mind is perfected to a greater degree, and has become polarized on the God of the universe, as was the mind of the Hebrew prophets, whose desire was to know the ultimate and future of this world, and the object of creation, then, musing upon the cause of the wonders of creation that we see around us, endeavoring to rise higher and higher, we shall get above this fermenting mass, and, as with them, so this imaging power that does its perfect work in nature will continue to do its perfect work in our brain. With them the life-forces were more and more perfected until they were so refined in their life that they could sense the very essence of the creative mind, — the mind of the great workman that we see forming and arranging and controlling this wonderful workshop, nature, and causing it all to work together toward one great object. Thus they, by constant meditation, were enabled to actually sense that mind, to actually collect and think the thoughts of this Infinite Soul, long years before they had wrought out their ultimation in physical form. For, through aspiration, they collected the creative thought; it took image in their brain, and was clothed like a seed with their essence, and prepared for its descent into matter, the same as a seed is clothed with a shell to prepare it for the earth. So the thought, emanating from the infinite mind, that was sent earthward to bring into the world an order of humanity who should enact certain parts in the great drama of life, in order to produce desired results upon this planet, was collected, imaged, and realized in their minds.

This imaging power of the brain, when once we are capable of sensing these infinite thoughts, will put them into their exact image, and there will be no mistake. They will accomplish their work; and, if we should live a thousand years, and at the end of that time see the image of our vision standing forth in human form, we would know it, and if we could have had a photograph taken from the image in our mind, we would say, "There is the picture, accurate; every part and particle of it is exact."

Again, we go among a class of people known as spiritualists, who have begun to feel after and inquire about these strange workings of the human mind. We go to a clairvoyant, and sit down before him or her, and they begin to tell us of the images that present themselves to their minds, and as they do so they attempt to explain them to us. Now, what is going on, and what is there real about it? You have around you certain mental conditions, perhaps the souls of some departed ones whose thought-potency clings closely to you. They sense it. They see forms standing before them and describe them perhaps accurately. By what means? By this imaging power of the brain. You take a letter, a lock of hair, a glove, a garment, that some loved and lost one has worn, take it to a psychognomist, who takes it in hand, and says, " I see such and such a one," drawing the picture, clear and unmistakable, of your lost one. " Yes, I know whom you mean; I know all about it; I know the person well; that was such a one."

What has taken place? Why, there was enough of the magnetic life-essences of the thought that had been formed in the life and action of that person, left attached on that garment to enable this sensitive brain to draw it in; and, as it did so, it would be able to see an unmistakable image of the wearer. This is a law of the infinite order that is active in us.

It is not every brain that perceives things or makes its images alike. As some have different functions, so this imaging power varies in different minds. Sometimes it is the order of sound, in others color (for order has a color, and color has an order, as we will see when we come to consider the cause of the seven colors). But, remember this, it is not necessary that we should have the soul of the departed come and present itself to the spiritual eye in order to see it; for we can prove by the glove or the garment that the image-power of the brain can take the little magnetic molecules of thought and give you the picture of the person from whose body they emanated. Here we see something of this divine mechanical power in each of us. It knows exactly what to do with every particle of this ethereal essence that comes in contact with us. It is a mechanic, indeed. It images a person, an animal, in an instant. It produces birds, reptiles, everything in its proper order.

The moment the element, the ether, if you please, whose nature it is to form such lives, comes in contact with the imaging power of the brain it makes it into the appropriate image in a minute: shall we say it deceives us? I think not. But, certainly, we could not make the image unless we had the proper material to work with. You can never see the image of your father, or your mother, or your daughter, by taking the glove or handkerchief that has been endowed with the magnetism of some other person, unless you do so by a thought projected from your own mind. The law of order in the mind of man works in exact accordance with the above rules. By tracing this law of order in its growth and unfoldment, and manifestation in the physical world, we have the explanation of all vision, of all these mystic and, at present, largely uncomprehended phenomena of the human mind. Here we will find the uses of thinking over the relations of these seven creative principles; for, remember this, friends, the God of creation does not deal with persons or things arbitrarily, but through the action and operation of these seven principles, which, in time, reveal their workings to the higher consciousness; this by virtue of constant practice, constant use, generation after generation, for ages up to the present time, has produced in us a certain likeness to the author-mind from whence we came; consequently, the mind begins to act like its parent, or, in other words, the man begins to look like his father; and Christ well says, "Call no man your father, for one is your father, even God." And here we find the first manifestation of the sixth sense, and of the God-principle in its sublimated expression of the law of order in the human mind; and it is in conformity with this law that mind acts on mind, and that, within certain limits, we have the power to appropriate or reenact the manifestations of the seven principles from our higher nature.

To a very great extent, in our large cities, we are in a sea of psychic influences from the masses, and to such an extent that it is only by a constant struggle or effort that we can act from our own nature; and the finer persons are, the more they are affected by the influences. We would be surprised, if we were separated from those altogether, at the change that would be produced; we would then discover how much we are acting from the influence of other minds. Persons who are fine and sensitive are often afflicted with disease through the controlling influence of low or evil-disposed persons; for, when the mind is under control of another, it affects the discriminating power of the digestion, and causes the persons to take into their circulation like elements to those who, for the time, control them; these elements are poison to them; thus disease is often produced, and sometimes death.

Humanity is involved in series, and stand intimately related each to the other, and thus we are constantly being acted upon by minds both above and beneath us; and, were we isolated from this magnetic relation with other minds, we would be astonished at finding how dependent the individual is; in fact, apart from the series of which we are an entity, individuality would be a mere cipher. We derive value and importance from discrimination and orderly adjustment and coherence to the force around, within, and above us, and may elect to work in a low or a high series the same as we discriminate and select in matters of diet and clothing; and this is a most important thought to keep in mind.

We may, therefore, be interiorly poisoned and paralyzed, or nourished and exalted, according to social, mental, and spiritual discrimination. These laws are absolute and eternal facts of nature, and cannot he controverted or ignored. Then why should we, as thinking men and women, when we see this law acting in this subtle manner in the human mind and nature, say it is all a delusion. We may delude ourselves with the phenomenon of the most simple things; but, when we stop and think, these are the means, this is the law, here is the power, and, according as we select, so are we servants or masters.

We are already joint-creators with the infinite mind. We are not conscious of it, because these creative energies that come from the infinite will come down to us through their successive stages, float through the successive degrees of mind and mechanical life, being fitted and prepared for their material use. Let us, then, begin to gather of the creative energy, and think its thoughts; and, as we do so, we throw off this surplus life, and animals and plants gather it up and make their bodies out of it, and so on, down and down, until it moves and moulds even gross matter. We stand here in this chain of existence, reaching from the Infinite Unknowable to the lowest, and every link of that chain is a stage of animate unfoldment. Man stands just between the animal and spiritual, or God-world, as we cull it; and, because of our capacity to feel, to see, and to handle those finer forces that are above and beyond us, they are just far enough so that we can reach and touch them, can receive of their thoughts, and then we bring them down into the lower faculties of our nature, and in turn aid those just below us, the higher faculties of whose being are capable of receiving these thoughts from us, and again carrying them down into the lower faculties of their nature, which are enabled to receive according to the uses and needs of their position.

We are standing in direct lineage to the God of the universe, being a joint-creator with him. All there is remaining for us to do is to go to work on self, clear away these gross elements of our being, get our minds refined, give the soul an opportunity to think and act freely, and then we will be enabled to follow the advice of the Nazarene when he said, "After this manner, pray." Yes, continually we will say, " Our Father, who art in heaven." But now, in this gross condition of the world, when none can realize spirit, — and God is spirit, — how then? Is it real, or is it hypocrisy, when we say, "Our Father, who art in heaven," and yet do not realize or believe it, when we have no idea of what spirit is, — no idea of that heavenly Father? Prayer is the sincere desire of the heart, the soul-yearning, the reaching out of the inner self towards something that it feels the need of. Can we truly feel the need of that we do not know anything about? Certainly not. The very foundation of the Christian religion demands that we should understand these laws and principles, and put them into practice, before we can take the first step in it, which is to "pray."

"When we recognize these things in the divine law of order, and our inner consciousness is open, so that the soul does actually recognize the source of its being, as the child recognizes its parent, its father, its mother. Then, with this evidence, it reaches up and says, "My Father, let thy kingdom come, that thy will may be done on earth as it is in the heavens," and is ready to labor for that ultimate in himself, and when all our thoughts and desires are concentrated on knowing the ultimate of this divine order on earth, we will possess the true Wisdom.

" I will be what I will to be."

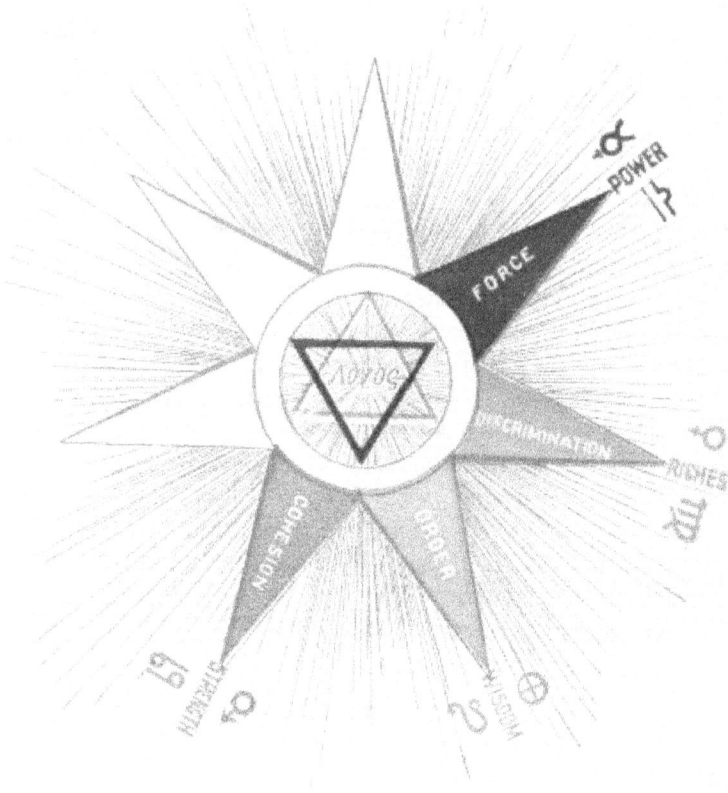

POWER

FORCE

DISCRIMINATION

RICHES

ORDER

CONFUSION

STRENGTH

FIFTH LECTURE. COHESION.

THE FOURTH OF THE SEVEN CREATIVE PRINCIPLES.

The subject for this evening's thought is Cohesion. I wish, before proceeding, to state certain facts necessary to give you some idea of our position. I find, by a careful analysis of my own personal experiences in the past, that I had no natural faculty for acquiring book-education, my chief love, from early childhood, being to read the great book of Nature, and, in my perusal of that book, the conclusions reached, I find, are identical with those of the old sages and philosophers, in regard to the creative principles; namely, that there are, in all, but seven principles that are operating in the realm of the earth, in the work of creation. Mark you, I am dealing with principles and not phenomena or materials.

We wish to distinguish, to draw the line carefully between principles and things. A principle is that interior potency that causes action and gives character, quality, and kind, when embodied in the conscious energy of man. Thus we can understand what is meant when we speak of principle. We often hear men say that they act from principle. Now, these are the creative principles that are active factors in the work of bringing up the lower conditions of matter to the higher conditions of manhood, in the work of evolution, — for we believe in evolution. We differ, perhaps, somewhat with Darwin and some others in the materialistic view of evolution. We do not believe in evolutionary unfoldment and stages of change through external and physical generation, but we believe in evolution of the mind, — of the more subtle principles of life. Everything in creation is aspiring to a stage above itself; and, when it has completed its experience and unfoldment upon one stage of existence, it, by the law of aspiration, reaches out to a higher stage of existence, in which it finds incarnation, and so the germ of life that now animates the blade of grass we tread upon, will, in some far-distant time in the future, be part of the mind that rules our planet Earth. This is the brief statement of my idea of evolution. We have, in the past, considered the idea of God, the cause and source of all being, which lecture should be read carefully, because without it you cannot form an adequate idea of the foundation upon which we are building; for we know that all religious systems and civilizations have been just what their idea of God was, let it have been what it may. Therefore, we find it to be absolutely necessary to make that thought the foundation on which to build. The second subject of consideration was the principle of force, which is magnetic and concentrative. The third lecture was a consideration of discrimination and polarization. The fourth treats of the law of order, which manifests itself in everything of form in Nature. This evening's thoughts will be on the principle of cohesion.

We considered, in our last lecture, the law of order, also the two other principles, the gathering and concentrating, and the discriminating power; we saw their manifestation in the frost-crystal upon the windowpane, which had, however, no true cohesive properties. As soon as warmth and sunlight came upon it, it was disintegrated and freed for another state of existence.

We have, to-night, to consider this fourth principle of Nature. Finding that the ancient philosophers gave us four general or universal "Elements" to start with, namely: lire, air, water, and earth, we have these four elements present and active in the earth; hut we shall treat them as effects rather than causes, and proceed with our consideration of cohesion, the fourth principle. To " cohere " implies the unity of the whole, to come together and adhere one to the other, to remain intact. Assisted by the other three primates, organic bodies spring into existence and adhere and remain in existence, go on in the work of gathering like substances around them, unfolding and manifesting themselves in their ultimates, and bringing forth their final fruits.

This fourth is the principle which expresses the idea of the mother-nature, and it may be carried from the lowest stage of maternal life to the highest that we can conceive of — spiritual motherhood. We hear the word frequently, " Theos Sophie," involving in it the dual relation of God as father and mother; this fourth principle is feminine, and we begin to consider it from that stand-point, drawing the line between the positive and negative; for we find that everything in Nature is either male or female, and that, as such, everything that belongs to life is dependent upon those two as factors of existence. Even the grass and all vegetation is thus known and accepted to be dual. It is also well known, that the first phase of organic life is almost invariably female. In some insect existences there are supposed to be at least two generations of the female before there is any male existence.

The female principle is that which nourishes, that holds together and encircles all things within its sphere. It protects and strengthens all things in Nature; and, as we look upon the animal world, we find the mother-nature possessed of two manifestations, — one of love and carefulness of its offspring, the other of defence, fury, and destruction to every invader. Therefore, wherever we find this principle manifest, we may expect these two extremes; and, in fact, everything in Nature exists by virtue of them. If we find a person or animate thing, let it be what it may, that manifests one principle in the extreme, it must of necessity have the opposite standing over against it, as a counterpoise in order to maintain its existence. This mother-principle is, in a degree, an adversary to the progressive unfoldment in Nature: yet it is the great friend to all that lives.

"We speak of the mother's love. "We magnify it in the highest degree. How carefully Nature everywhere guards her young! How eagerly she reaches out the hand to gather the supplies necessary for their wants! How vigilant in looking after and protecting her own! But were it not for an adversary that is equally potent in nature we never should have been here. Were it possible that this principle of cohesion which gathers, forms, and maintains, had not an equal set over against itself, there would be no change throughout all time.

I called attention, the other evening, to the fact that this mother-nature was one of instinct rather than reason. It loves its offspring, the object of its care, no matter what it may be. Not only so, but I have heard mothers who have an over-endowment of this mother-nature in them, say, "I wish baby could always remain just as he is." It came as a thought and desire that the child should never unfold beyond its childhood, so that she might always have it in her arms, and be always in the exercise of motherly care.

Let us think of this mother-principle standing out distinct, alone in human form. This principle that thus holds and preserves and cares for all things in Nature, is the principle we so much admire. There are two reasons why this is so. One is, that by nature, all animal life loves ease; it does not like to struggle for self-preservation, it wants to be at ease, and this mother-principle is struggling to give rest and comfort; therefore we love it, and we magnify it as something good, as being superior to the other seven principles. Our next lesson will bring us to consider the adversary of this mother-nature, "the Serpent," "the Devil," we have heard so much about; and it may surprise you to hear that this is one of the seven creative principles, and that it is just as necessary as the mother-nature. This mother-nature which we love, being conservative of present conditions, becomes adverse to every effort on the part of human intelligence to break through old conditions and rise into a new sphere of thought, life, and action, and thus it becomes an adversary. Jesus said, when he was here, "that a man's foes should be they of his own household," and it is wholly because of this principle being the controlling one.

We must also consider this principle jointly with its companion, that we treated of in the previous lectures. This mother-nature inspheres in its action the positive principle, the principle of order. It holds and limits this divine activity, puts the material that has been gathered into form, holds and maintains this form, which, having in it also the active principles of force and discrimination, struggles for a manifestation in a broader and higher career. This is inevitable, because the negative principle of Nature has gathered in and insphered the object of its love. It is the divine masculinity that this cohesive principle has insphered and bound within its own limits; therefore, this captive life, this divine masculinity is restive and active to develop and come forth into a higher, broader, and better order of

Nature, which can only be done through unfoldment from the innermost to the external, on account of the cohesive and binding properties of the mother-nature.

When we examine a plant we find that this principle of cohesion compacts and holds it, giving it a hard, solid stalk. It stands, perchance, with two branches, as if it were to remain there to all eternity; but a more subtle principle is ever working from the innermost, projecting from between its two branches another that grows out from the centre; and, as it unfolds, it expands the confines of its position, that it may have room to manifest itself; and when it has burst its bonds, the mother-nature, being ever active, lays hold and concentrates her energy on the new branch that is just forming, and as she gathers material to support, nourish, and preserve, she is inclined to overfeed her young. We never knew a mother, no matter in what kingdom, whether in the plant-world or in the more perfect state of human existence, who was not inclined to overfeed her young. She always keeps gathering and gathering; for preservation is her attribute. It is the principle that is most active to-day among men, and that is cursing our land. The disposition to gather, heap up, and hoard millions of treasure, without stopping to ask the question, what use they will be to them.

We are acting under these blind forces of Nature, and never stopping to think what their qualities are, and therefore we are struggling all the time, and combating one with the other without any reason or judgment; thus this divine principle for the preservation of all things becomes an adversary because of abuse and overdoing. Thus, in all the workings of Nature, the best things, when misused, become the very worst things, as instanced in the Lord's saying, "that a man's foes should be of his own household."

This mother-nature is supposed to maintain and hold all things as they are, to preserve and maintain present conditions. It looks back and sees what has been. It acts from its own present status, without any regard to the thought that is beyond. While this principle controls the home, family, and public mind, as it does today, every advanced thought that comes into our minds will be opposed by our friends, by those who love us most, especially if that advanced thought necessitates any change on our part. Here again we find we are led to struggle against the very things that we love the most, — the principle that conserves our lives, that maintains our existence, as if it were our adversary; otherwise we would be bound and held by it, and be unable to move forward in any direction. It is for that reason that Jesus, the. master, said, "that unless a man hate father, mother, wife, and children, yea, and his own life," he could not be his disciple. For this law is one that is absolute, acting in life everywhere.

I called your attention, in the early part of the lecture, to the fact that each one of those seven principles may have the dominancy and be found the specially active one; but none of the seven can act alone. All must co-work with it. But we can consider some one as the leader in the action, and we must consider each in their sphere of leadership, and how the action results, so that we may know how to subject these powers and bring them under control of our will, and make them useful factors in our life. These thoughts are for the purpose of giving an understanding of these seven primate laws of Nature, so that each of you may, by their own will, take control of them, and become master of the work. As we announced at the beginning, the thought in the Infinite Mind was to make man in his image and likeness, and lot them have dominion; and, in order to do so, we must have knowledge of these laws, and when we have, we may lay hold upon them and resist their control, accept of their assistance, and move on in harmony, not allowing eccentricities to carry us beyond the bounds of reason.

If we look into the workings of Nature, as I have previously shown you, everything is based on the duality of sex. This fourth principle cohesion, being the mother-principle, is peculiarly the love-principle, the magnetic, and if we love a person we know that we will do everything in our power for their good as we understand it.

Now the mother-nature, considered as a distinct principle, has no reason. The law of order in the pure mother-principle has no place. The feminine principle, as manifested in the higher order of womanhood, is not a reasoning principle, but it acts from the spontaneous soul, from within. It acts from the law of its nature, and we call it intuition. Intuition, when governed by cohesion, struggles against human progress. If you have a son; and that son has an inclination to a life that is not according to the life your father lived, not according to that you yourself are living, you at once condemn it, and at once begin to struggle against it. If a man or woman attempts to live on a different plane of existence from that on which you are, you condemn it, and do all in your power to hold on to that friend, and bind him in the sphere of your own existence. These are thoughts that we ought to think about, because we are in the time of progress. We have nearly finished a cycle of the earth's unfoldment. What do I mean by "cycle"? We all understand what a cycle of the earth's revolution around the sun means. It means spring-time, the time of planting, mid-summer, the fullness of growth, the time of harvest, and of winter, the time of cold, when all things congeal, when the chilling blasts blight all vegetable life. This we understand to be a cycle of earth. Human life is of the same order. The Nazarene, and all the ancient prophets and sages delighted in that as a figure. " The seed-time and harvest of the world." We have a history of this world, supposed to be for about six thousand years. Back of that we have but very little knowledge; some nations traced much farther back; but the knowledge is vague and uncertain, and all so different from the experience of these six thousand years that it bears every resemblance of belonging to another time, to ages or cycles different from ours. But we have now come near to the closing scenes of another cycle. Human life today is struggling with an energy never before manifested in the history of the world. The mind of man is reaching out for knowledge in every direction. New thoughts are being gathered in, and new unfoldments and new conditions are demanded; and, by virtue of this we find that the mother-principle is becoming an adversary in our midst, and we are forced to become positive to it. Think of it, an adversary to our mother! That which brought us into being; that which has preserved us, given us our life! What a cruel heart it must require! Yet, what shall we do? The very object in the mind of the great parent of all life that organized these forms of maternal nature, was that you should break away from that condition of environment, and arise into a higher condition, — into one broader, more useful, more characteristic of that divine nature of which you are the expression.

Let us look at this from another stand-point. We read the ancient cabala, and find much about the " Elementals." We find that nearly all the ancient philosophers taught a great deal about the elementals of Nature. (However, they made a distinction between elementals and elementaries, at least some of them did.) What are these elementals? We have them described to us as being of four different natures; the nature of fire, the nature of air, the nature of water, and the nature of earth. They also, as they come nearer to earth and its atmosphere, combine the pure elements of air with that of fire, and that of water, and, finally, with that of the earth. These combinations are also described as having forms like men, very beautiful, very wise. We have heretofore been trying to present to you the idea of what our thoughts are. That our thoughts are our children, born of our conceptive intellect, born of the materials of our body, through this intellect or brain, projected out from us by the will, sent into the ether. The fine sensitives see them, absorb them into their brain, interpret them, even describing their author. Perchance my thoughts may be gathered and interpreted by those that never saw me, and they may describe me just as I am speaking to you to-night. These elementals that have been seen by the clear-eyed seer of the past are thoughts generated from the creative mind; and, as they come nearer and yet nearer, they begin to take more and yet more of the earth-conditions. These thoughts have descended into earth; and the mother-principle, which is the earth-principle, has laid hold upon them, and insphered them in living forms, covered them with substance, and preserves and holds them in earth-bondage. Such are the souls of men that have come up through the successive stages of earth-existence to where we are to-day. These are not uncreated beings, as thought by many of the ancient philosophers, but they are created. The same as I am this moment creating thought-forms and sending them out into this room, so, too, the Soul of the Universe is constantly creating thought-forms. Yea, the planetary worlds, in their revolutions and relations one to the other, are creating thought-forms and concentrating a share of them upon the planet earth. These, through the agency of this fourth principle, are being laid hold upon and incarnated in material bodies.

The office of this mother-principle is to preserve and hold spirits in material bodies. That is why the ancient philosophers said it was impossible for woman to become a master, because her nature was that which took hold of, and bound all things in the flesh, and would not admit of that unfoldment that led into the spirit and the transmutation of the flesh. Therefore, they said, it was an absolute necessity that woman should go down to the grave and return as man in the second incarnation; for it was so believed by them. (For instance, you who to-day are here as women, the next time you will return as men. Again, you pass away and return as women, and so on, alternately. This is in harmony with the law of reincarnation. In connecting 1 these subjects I am necessitated to throw out many things that may seem vague and unreasonable to those "who have not thought deeply on such subjects, too great to expound in a single lecture. This is a new field of thought to the Occident, but not to the Orient.)

"Woman has got to stop and think and try to unite her soul with the great Mother of the Universe. She has got to begin to look at herself and her companion, not as flesh, not as body, or as mere material. As long as she does, just so long will she be an adversary, and so long she herself will be bound in earth and will know nothing of the higher life, and the object of her love, because of that flesh she loves and clings to, will struggle against her, and slip out of her hands, and she will be found deserted and alone. The time has come when that mother-love must begin to take higher form. The divine Mother loves all her children alike, and so woman has to consider all as her children, all as objects of her special care and protection, and the husband as counterpart of her spirit, and not merely of the flesh, and that this spirit is a part of her spirit and as such it must be the object of her love, the object that she must try to aid, to unfold, and to free from its encumberings of earth. That, you see, at once reverses all the action of the old love-life. That is a question that she must consider. For, as long as the action of her present life is that manifestation that belongs to cohesion alone, it is holding the persons she loves; it is binding their thought, consequently hindering their action, and keeping them just as they are.

Should this principle of cohesion have sway from this time, all would stop thinking and acting. Everything would be at a dead stand-still. We bless that divine principle; we should, and do admire and adore the mother-love. Yet, while it is good, it is good only while it is useful. There is nothing permanent that does not serve a use. Keep this maxim ever before you, that the great law of the Infinite Mind is that the use of a thing determines whether it is good or not. Now, when as mothers, as wives, those of you

51

whose natures are overflowing with that divine maternal principle, and who have looked higher, deeper, more into the real man and the real woman, have discerned that a man is not the flesh, but the spirit, the soul, then will you begin to find that your relation to him is the relation of one-half of his being, and that Paul had in mind a law which is beyond that understood to-day when he said, ' f The man is not without the woman or the woman without the man in the Lord." Therefore the first thing to do is to conquer self, conquer this maternal nature in its lesser manifestations. Mothers and sisters, conquer yourselves! Men and brothers, rise above it; do not allow it to hinder your progress! Some may say, " "Why, what will this do; where will it lead us? " It will lead you into new and higher conditions. Remember this: if, for the time being, it does cost you a struggle, caused by misunderstandings, live up to your highest ideal of right; do not think that you are injuring any one, though it may appear so for a time. Suppose you should sit down, each one of you, because this one or that one says you are eccentric, and, therefore, submit to this mother-principle that holds you, year after year, in what would it result? In the end it Mould make you a burden upon those loved ones, whereas, if you, like the man who has fallen in the mire, rise up, notwithstanding the remonstrance of your fellow, rise up out of it yourself, you get on a solid foundation, and then reach down and help your companions. The mission of this world requires action. We cannot stand still where we are; we must go forward, and the only method for us, men or women, is: First, go to work in accordance with the higher idea of right in yourself, live up to your highest ideal; and, when you have done that, you will find yourself placed on a solid foundation, upon high ground where you can help those who are trying to hinder you. That is how you should "love your enemies, bless them that persecute, and do good to them that hate and despitefully use you," "because they know not what they do."

There is not a man or woman in the world who is intentionally and wholly evil. They have a law of right that seems to justify their action. "When we look at these things from the stand-point of law we will find that it is difficult to blame any one for the things he does. But, on the contrary, when we see persons so low down in darkness, and so overwhelmed by some one of these seven principles, that they can see nothing beyond it, we sympathize with them, and, in the same degree that we have ourselves made attainments and taken control, we will have power to lift the load from our fellow that is being crushed by it, let it be our wife, our husband, our son, our daughter, a comrade, or a stranger, or any man or woman that lives. Let us lift the burden, and help them on their journey.

Just as soon as we allow one feeling of hatred to come into our heart against any thing or person, their ignorance has control of us, and that moment we become an adversary perhaps to their higher good, and certainly to our own. Such thoughts take form and go out and become an active factor to create adversaries that tear and rend us. For they do not always destroy the object of their hate; but such thoughts often go out and unite with others, and cause the object of the hatred to generate a multitude of like thoughts, and send them back upon us for our destruction. However, while this mother-nature on the lower plane is evil, when it has taken its place in proper harmony in the truly united man and woman it becomes the source of strength, as it restrains the positive nature of man from rashness and violence, and concentrates all the forces, puts them under control of the will. And this will is the only principle that enables us to take the name of God, place it "in our forehead" (the seat of intelligence), and to say, "I will be what I will to be," thus lifting the principle of cohesion to its ultimate, which is "Strength."

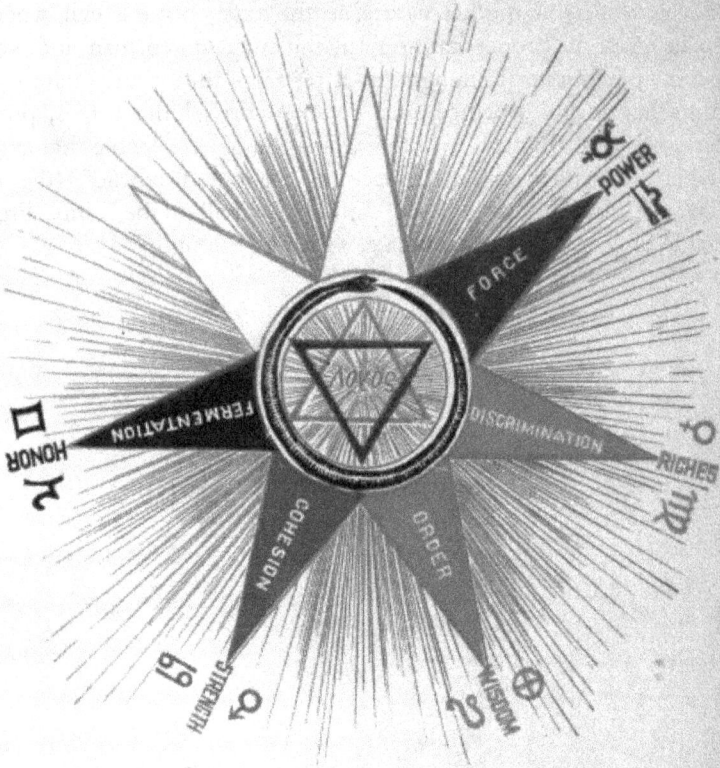

יהוה

"I will be what I will to be."

54

SIXTH LECTURE. FERMENTATION.

THE FIFTH OF THE SEVEN CREATIVE FRINCIFLES.

"We are brought this evening to the consideration of the fifth principle of creative energy. We have in the past considered, first, force, that which is the cause of action and also the cause of negation; second, discrimination, which distinguishes and causes everything to seek its kind; the third is order, which is that wondrous mechanic, so faithfully performing his duty in building everything in the world into variety and beauty of form, as we everywhere behold; fourth, cohesion, the mother-principle that we so love and venerate, and which works so faithfully in preserving, holding, and maintaining all things that have been brought into existence by the three prior forces. Now we come to the fifth principle; and let us for a moment consider the world, when all Nature is in full bloom, vegetation and animation beaming with life and beauty. This life and beauty would be immortal, unchangeable, were it not for the fifth principle, which comes in as a destroyer, to tear down that which has fulfilled its use, to scatter its parts, and, at the same time, to prepare for another state of existence where its atoms may return again, each to their own appointed further uses.

This, being the fifth principle, it is, consequently, stronger than any of those which have preceded it, therefore we find ourselves in a domain of struggle. This fifth principle has been represented to us from the time of antiquity as the old Serpent, the Devil, and Satan, that deceiver of the world. There are many reasons for this. First, that in the fall of the year, as the leaves fall, vegetation is cut off and the rain carries these leaves and decaying matter down into the swamps where fermentation holds its court and has its sway. The life essences that caused the vegetation and matured its existence are there brought within the province of the adverse principle of life; a struggle goes on and throws off unfit matter; and life itself, being immortal, Gathers itself into a new form. The first form of animation which is thus brought into existence by fermentation is that of the insect, reptile, and serpent. We find that the same law obtains in the first phase of life in the water, which is in the form of the reptile. In fact, the first form of everything that has life, ourselves included, in germ state, is that of the reptile, and these first forms of life always appear in that department of our nature or physical structure which answers to and is characterized by the principle of fermentation. We have observed and may have read that in autumn, as vegetation is decaying, there are great quantities of flies and insects in the air; at times the air seems to be literally filled with them, and the solution is given that we are having a great deal of decomposition of vegetation, and therefore these flies and insects. That is true, but by what

55

law does the decaying vegetation bring these insects into existence? The life in the plant is immortal as much as the life in you or me, but it is in a crude state of being. We take it and analyze it. We extract the chemical essences and name the chemical qualities of which that plant is composed. We may bring it down to the quintessence of those qualities, and we find its power of chemical combination; how it may form the most powerful agents by its many strong properties that produce strange results when brought in contact with other chemicals, and, at this present stage of chemistry, after analyzing and extracting the qualities of plant life, we give them names according to the rules of chemistry. But we stop there; we are not educated to think that these chemical substances have anything in them of life, simply because our chemistry to-day is not perfected to trace far and deep enough to find the thought-essence that brought that plant into being.

You will remember that in our earlier considerations of this chart we called attention to the word " Logos " in the centre, which carried us back to the Bible where John, who is accredited as being a cabala student, said, " In the beginning was the Word and the Word was with God and the Word was God," or, in the more critical rendering, " and the Word was with Power and the Word was Power, and that all things were made by it, and without it was not anything made that was made." The "Word" is a thought formed out of the essences of the person or thinker, as we have shown you before, which is proved in Psychogonomy. Every plant and vegetable that grows is a thought-form from the mind of the thinker; the life essences have proceeded from that thinker. The same element of life that gave us birth, that gave animation to the germ from which we came; and, if that germ had been retained in the body, it would have been transmuted and called up to the brain, — would have been the element for thought-forms that would have came forth instead. Our thoughts are as much our children as the physical children that are born to us in the marital relation. So, also, is vegetation the thought-forms of the Infinite Mind. The grass on which we unthinkingly tread will yet become the people that will walk this earth in time to come, — the men and women that take our place.

Thus the life-essence that forms grass and all vegetation is the essence of the Thinker, and when this principle of fermentation lays hold upon it, that essence being endowed with higher life, struggles to maintain its existence.

We find in all Nature, and especially in our own existence, that we have to struggle to maintain our standing among the living, and how hard it often is for us to get the necessary food to supply the exhaust due to the anxiety and restlessness of our life-energy! These are some of the struggles we experience in our own personal efforts against this adversary and destroyer.

Now, in the action of the plant, this life-essence concentrates, unites its forces, to become new organic life. So, again, the mother, when she is pressed to an extreme in the preservation of her children from some enemy, how quickly she gathers them and puts her arms around them and holds them together! So this maternal principle in the action of fermentation, when life is about to be thrown off into gases, and the last remains of its forms to be scattered, concentrates the germs of its being, and at once formulates, out of the scattering essences of the plant, living organisms, built together according to the polarity of the atoms, according to the necessity and character of the body, worm or insect existence, or whatever its qualities may be. For every plant has its own leading chemical qualities which determine what kind of an insect it will be that comes forth from it, and when we have gone farther on in our studies of this wonderful law of order in Nature so that we shall be as wise as those who have passed into the eternal world, and need no other language but the actual form of the thing, we will be able to know when we sec those little insect-forms the exact chemical properties of which they are composed. But not only that, but we shall know also the exact thought that they are the formation of, and again we shall know that the essences of that plant, when once extracted, brought down to the very quintessence of its nature, will be substance, which, brought in contact with man, will produce a thought in him exactly characterized by its nature, so that the art of mental healing will some day have also a system of chemistry. For as long as generation abounds in the world, while this law of fermentation controls, sickness will exist, until man has learned the chemistry of Nature as well as the law of mind, for the two belong together, and when we have learned just what thought is embodied in each plant, our faculties being sufficiently refined, we can draw and take from them the very essences of thought and apply them. A change of mind is directly produced, and the disease will be healed. This is no new idea, however. It is the thought of the alchemists of antiquity, and was known long ages ago, though the knowledge was kept in great sacredness by the old Magi, because if this knowledge was given to the public great harm would have come of it. These subtle essences of plants may be so refined that even a touch would change the whole mental condition of a person. For instance, I have read, of late, of an axe-handle being made hollow, and in the open space there was placed a certain chemical essence. It had been there a great while, yet every one that took that axe in his hand was filled with a desire to murder his best friend; and, finally, an attempt was made to carry it out; through accident the handle broke, and the secret was discovered. Such are the stories which are brought down to us from antiquity; they are not without foundation. All these powerful essences are found and obtained through the law of fermentation.

Fermentation, again, finds its locality in the places where the old must be torn down, and where a new and higher organism must be built up. In one way it is an adversary, a devil, an evil one; one to be struggled against;

on the other hand, it is a benefactor. Therefore you see that in everything in Nature there is nothing that lives, no principle, but what is good. We are again brought to the maxim that the greatest evil, when inverted, is the greatest good. We are told that without fermentation the food would never digest. Without fermentation of the body there would be no germs of new life formed. Without fermentation in the world, we are brought to say again, everything would remain as it is. Now, this fermentation does not stop with merely the tearing down of decaying vegetation, but in everything that dies fermentation comes as a liberator of the forces. If circumstances are favorable, so that the liberated, life-essences can come forth in the form of worms or insects, they will be formed; if not, then those life-essences are sent out into the elements and again become parts of the forces of nature called " elementals." These elementals have been, to all philosophers, a great mystery in Nature. We hear of late much said about the elementals and the elementary spirits. What are they? We are taken back for an answer to the word we have just called your attention to, "Logos," the Word of God, the thought-emanation which is sent from the mind of the Creator earthwards; and to the fact that these thoughts appear to the clairvoyant eye in the form of the thinker. You all know and remember if you take a glove or handkerchief and put it in the hands of the psychognomist, though she may never have seen the one who wore it, she holds it and sees the image of the wearer and describes him accurately to you. So, when man is sufficiently unfolded from within, and his finer nature takes cognizance of the forces in Nature, his clairvoyant eye takes cognizance of these thought-formations. He comes into communication with them by the same method as the psychognomist does.

Some time ago I called your attention to the law by which the ancient Hebraic prophecies were formed. How that the masters of antiquity, devout ones who gave their lives to knowing the will and the mind of God the creator, clearly saw it was necessary for them, in order to be able to collect and understand the mind of God, to isolate themselves from the public. They lived in dens and caves in the wilderness and desert places where no man could penetrate and find them, dwelling constantly in the contemplation of the cause-world and of the God of the universe, holding and maintaining their own life-forces, carrying on the work of the regeneration and refinement of their own inner mind-power. They went on and on, until they began to take cognizance of the mind of the Creator. They saw in the angel-forms that appeared to them the thoughts of God descended to earth and having in them all the elements of the Infinite Spirit, the spirit of the God of creation, that had formed the thought and sent it earthward to gather to itself all the elements, first of fire, then of air, of water, of earth, and finally be immersed in vegetable formations on the earth. From these the pure essences of being would be gathered up by the animal, taken into his chemical laboratory and formed into flesh; and again a higher order of animals would come and feed on his flesh, carrying this life on, higher and higher, from the little insect, born and perishing in a day, up to the highest order of man. The ox goes to the grass. He gathers there the life-essences. "We eat the flesh of the ox and take his life-essences into our own body, and formulate with them what are called elementals. They have not been understood, and I have never found evidence yet that any of even the Cabalists, or Oriental philosophers, knew what these spirit-forms, as they appeared to them, were. They found out this much, — that they disappeared, that they seemingly did not live forever, and went somewhere, but where they could not tell. But we know from the law of creation that these pure elementals, pure as the God himself, when starting from the Infinite Mind, came down, down, down through the multifarious changes, until final by they stand here as an incarnate mind, ascending again to the cause from whence we came, these elementals being the animating principle of our body.

It is the spirit of life that makes us men and women, thinking and reaching out for higher and grander things. That life was once that pure element that floated in the ether; it was once that bright Sylph that floated in the air; the Salamander that flashed through the flames, clothed with its elements; that pure Nymph that lived in the element of water, and, again, that Gnome that lived in the earth. These are the four kinds of spiritual elements, and in these four there are multifarious stages. Now, then, these life-giving elementals, finding their incarnation merely in the earth and vegetable, were it not for this fifth principle of fermentation where would they be to-day? where would we be? Not here, no; but we are here by virtue of the faithful performance of the duty, or the faithful acting out of the nature of the old Serpent, the Devil, the opposer of human life and of the perpetuity of all formation that is.

That same principle of fermentation exists in our minds. The lower nature, we say, must not control. If the lower nature control, then we become combative, destructive, disposed to find fault with and combat our fellows, and to be restless and dissatisfied. It is because that principle is a warring one, it is a struggling adversary ever ready to kill, to tear down and to destroy. It is the principle, too, of anger. It is said if a cat is made very angry her bite is almost equal to that of a mad dog, and have you not noticed in persons of a very intense nature, when they are angry, how changed their eyes are, how much like the glassy eyes of the serpent that seem to pierce you through. There, again, the fermentative principle has risen up and taken control of the man or woman, and the serpent and destroyer is the master, and rules the body. And what chemical change is going on in the body while that rules? Could you again come into that interior state where your spirit eyes were open, and see these bare elements of Nature, you would see around that man, and, emanating from his words, dragons and reptiles of the most terrible forms coming forth out of his mouth and even pendant from his hair and from every part of his body! That poisonous chemical essence, coming in contact with the nature of sensitive persons, causes an intense chemical action there and brings on many diseased conditions, especially with our women, in whom this fermentative principle is so active; it is that very thing that the women of to-day should investigate. It is noted that there is scarcely one of our American ladies thoroughly healthy in the reproductive functions, because of the excited, active, combative state of our people. The fermentative principle is active, and it lays hold of and destroys the very fountain of their being. "We know when we go on further that man cannot live without woman, and that man, whose sphere it is to go out into the world and battle in business, and act, labor, and struggle, draws his energy and power from the woman, for she is the tree of life from which he obtains inspiration and power. I have watched men for many years in their habits of life and business, and I can tell you what kind of a wife a man has from his business habits. By seeing a wife I can tell you what kind of a business man her husband is, because I see the nature of the chemical fountain, and know what it will produce.

When the fermentative principle dominates man, as it does to-day, he is angry at once with the least thing; he is excitable and ready to combat instantly, because of the forces stored up by the old serpent. It rules him; it is tearing down his body and scattering it to the winds. This waste of his life is creating those worms that are destroying our vegetation. It is causing the destructive insect-existences that till the air with poisoning fungus causing many forms of disease.

Could we look into Nature we would deem it a wonder that man or woman can exist in our cities, beset as they are on every side by such terrible spiritual agents. These are the works of fermentation. What shall we do? As wise men we have got to go back and begin at the fountain of being, the sex-function, which embodies that principle of fermentation, and take control of it, subdue it, and rule it, by a wise and exalted mind.

Our Mother Church has made an effort to cut off one of the main branches in that direction. It teaches us that when we get angry we do wrong, and must conquer our lower nature. This is an effort to cut off some of the tops, but it does not go down to the root. Jesus, the Great Master, and whom I adore as such, says, "Behold the axe is laid at the root of the tree and every tree that bringeth not forth good fruit is hewn down and cast into the fire." To lay the axe at the root of the tree is to lay it at the root of our being, at the very fountain-head of our existence, the very source from whence we came. There the old Serpent has his home, there the creator Elohim, the power over generation, yes, the power with which Jacob wrestled and which he conquered; — then said the angel to Jacob, '

Thy name is no longer Jacob, but shall be called Israel," that is, "Prevailing Prince." "For now thou hast power with God and man and thou shalt prevail." He laid the axe at the root of the tree. He struggled with the God of creation, the God of generation, the God that has created all things. For all things are created through the functions of generation, even the sands on which we walk were once the living, animated bodies of fish and animals of the sea and earth. We are walking constantly on the ashes of the dead. There are no other solids but what have come into being by that principle of generation. Here is the God of creation, and we have known him in this function only as of the devil. "We have hated him and loved him. We have spurned him and we have drawn him to us. We have called him evil and we have enthroned him in dominion over our lives. These are the workings of humanity in their ignorance of law.

Now, you see that it is necessary that we should begin to think, in order that we begin to assert our rights as sons of God, to know something about these laws that govern our being. And when we do understand them, we will see that it is not sacrilege to say that " I will be what I will to be." Nothing more than saying what was said in the ancient Scripture, " God will not hold him guiltless that taketh his name in vain." His name, which is "Yahveh," meaning, "I will be what I will to be." "That is my name forever," said He to Moses, "and that is my memorial to all ages." Who can say, "I will be what I will to be"? Yet we have got to step out in the dignity of our divine sonship and say to the god of generation, to this creative destroyer that is active in us, that is destroying our bodies for the sake of our offspring, " I will no longer be subject to your law. I will be what I will to be, and you. shall serve my will." Thus, like Jacob, we shall wrestle with this sex-principle where life is generated and that should be utilized in perfecting and unfolding our life-forces, giving power and animation to our bodies.

Many say "this cannot be," but you have only to look into your own families. You have one son, who through some mental condition, perhaps, that was active in your mind at the time of conception, created in him a desire to control these forces. He is never led into any abusive habits, and you will see him grow and develop, broad-shouldered, a noble form of manhood and strength, with red cheeks and bright eyes. The other son, through some thoughtlessness on your part, has been endowed with that inflamed passion. He has abused and wasted those forces. You see in him a narrow chest and shoulders, a dwarfed body, pale cheeks, dull, watery eyes, a mere pigmy of a man beside the brother. Why? Because he has wasted the very elements that should have been used to make him a grand man. The other cherished them, and now when he comes to manhood, if he knew this divine law, he could become like Jacob, "a Prevailing Prince." The law is not a new one, it was carried out by the masters of antiquity. It has been known from the history of the world. By conquering and controlling that function, that power, saying to the old serpent, "You are my servant," you put the heel of your foot upon his head, and then, in the dignity of your manhood, you will become master and head of that power, thus making this most destructive principle, this "old serpent," this adversary of all right, this destroyer of all existence, this father of all sin, of all evil, your obedient servant.

The sex principle is now the master of the world. It rules all men; it rules from the highest down to the lowest grades of mankind, and how does it rule? Observe the ruin. Look back over the history of the world and behold our earth running with blood like streams of water; it was that old serpent's rule that did it. And that old serpent is the adversary that comes in between the beloved wife and her husband. They marry, they know nothing but purity. The wife, from her childhood pure as the angel spirit from whence she came, with her forces all turned toward the brain, all serving to the finer works of the spirit, loving with a pure and angelic love, that gives herself, soul and body and mind, to the object of her love. lie, on the other hand, with his admiration and animation, being attracted by that fountain of pure love, draws it to him and finally, when they come into that most sacred relation, devoid of that true knowledge, being taught nothing by you, parents, who have let that principle rule unrestrained, becomes the swift destroyer of the pure love he has won, converting it into an adversary that makes of his home a hell, transforming that pure and divine love into a demon that cares and struggles only for self-gratification. Where is that loving family, that beautiful home, that ideal companion, that was so beautiful a picture in the maiden's mind, that lived and grew in the mind of the young man? Where has it gone? What was the cause of it? The old serpent, the principle of fermentation and destruction, has done it; but only and simply because we have not known how to use this principle. We have not stopped to think that we should teach our young men and women that this principle has a specific use, and that we should be the master and have the say and control. We turn and look upon the animal world. By what means do they know? Because they have never yet begun to reason, therefore they live and act from the Solar mind. They utilize their forces for reproduction alone, and no more. They know where to go and get their food, how to protect themselves, because their life is still purely under the control of the invisible mind.

"We read that strange history of Adam in the garden of Eden. Eden means chaste, pure pleasure. He was in that pure state of pleasure. He had followed the thought of the instinctive, or intuitive mind. By the leading of that mind, the powers had unfolded within him, and finally he came to discern the divine law, and be led by it; for, remember, we started out by telling you that the original thought that made this world, — of which all the chemical essences are constituted, — was to make a world, people it with men, and with men that should be in the likeness and image of the Creator. Everything in Nature, the element of the solar fluid, and all the world, is teeming with that thought. Animals, birds, insects, and everything, are diligently at work everywhere lo carry out their part of the great work. Adam was led by it up to the point of time where he began to use his reason in opposition to his soul's intuitive guidance, and as soon as he refused to obey the commands of the soul, he fell. His power was gone, he was plunged into darkness, into uncertainty. Long ages of struggling, ambitious reasonings and combatings followed, wherein the old serpent, this sex and creative principle, has held the rod of government as a monarch ruling over all the earth, even up to the present day. Now we have come to a time when reason is being spiritualized; it is being called upon to unite with intuition, and to know why these things are so, by what laws they have been, and what methods it is necessary to apply in order to rise up and take control of them. Therefore, we adopt the words of Jesus and " lay the axe at the root of the tree," and begin at the principle of generation. We begin by taking control of that function, regenerating ourselves, perfecting our bodies, becoming god-men and god-women, so that we may come into our inheritance that was prepared for us from the foundation of the world. Being king's and priests unto God, reigning on the earth, and thus obtaining the ultimate of this principle, which is "Honor."

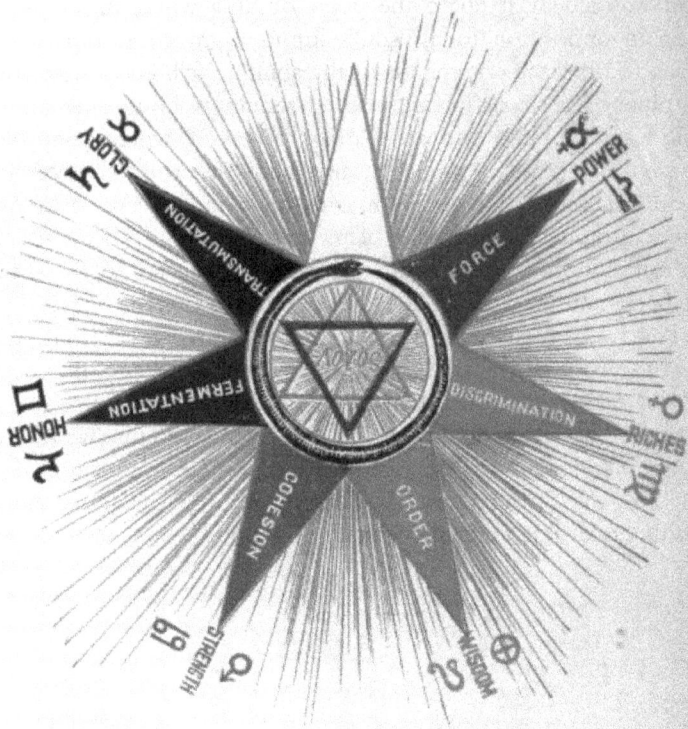

64

SEVENTH LECTURE. TRANSMUTATION.

THE SIXTH OF THE SEVEN CREATIVE PRINCIPLES.

The subject for this evening's consideration is fitly expressed by a simple illustration, like this lighted match. The solid substances here are transmuted into gases by what we caliber. This work is transmutation. It is the sixth of the seven creative principles. The first four bring into existence, formulate, and maintain organic life. The fifth, as you have been shown, is the adversary of all organic life that is formed; and not only the adversary, but the tearer down of the unfit. I called your attention, some time ago, to that peculiar function, the mother-principle, cohesion; how it binds, and inspheres, and holds in bondage, the elements collected by the first principle, force. In the fifth principle, fermentation, we find a means of the liberation of the divine essence that has been collected and bound and caused to be a servant to Nature. Its main office is that of a destroyer, and finds its expression in those principles of nature that we have already demonstrated as being the adversary, the devil. The sixth brings us to the principle of fire, transmutation.

The ancient Cabala has much to say of the Salamander. Strange stories are told of these beautiful creatures; for they are not hideous, as we have had them pictured to our minds by the ignorant and unlearned in these subjects, but most beauteous creatures to human perception. These beautiful thought-forms of the creative mind descend, and are absorbed in Nature, and give vitality and vivacity to the lower creations, which we call inanimate matter. Although we realize, when we begin to examine Nature, that there is no such thing as absolute inanimation; everything is animate, living, and acting, teeming with life, not only in earth-forms, in their multifarious conditions, microscopic and gigantic; but, when our eye becomes clear, and the inner senses are opened, we also see that what we call space, is teeming with life, whose forms are far more varied than those w-e see with the ordinary eye; all emanations from the one great centre of Cause.

I told you in our last lecture that the fourth principle brings us to vegetable life, and the fifth produces the first phase of animal life, in which sensation is only borrowed. No matter in what way it appears, sensation is a form of thought, and in this lower order of creation it is thought belonging to the great Soul of the Universe, and acts from the mind of that Soul according to its own qualities; for as soon as an organism is formed there is always something ready in Nature to animate it. If conditions are ready for an organic body, that divine life that permeates all things will animate it, and make it an individualized existence.

When we look for this principle of transmutation down in the first forms of animate life, we see but dim shadowings of its action. The only phase of manifestation there is in the power that the creatures possess of reproducing their kind, and also of taking nourishment into the body and transmuting the incorporated elements to finer substances that are adapted to the needs of the organized body. For as soon as the little insect that comes from decaying and fermenting vegetation comes upon the stage of action it begins to feed upon the emanations from the parent plant. It receives strength sufficient to begin to act independent of its surroundings, according to its quality.

The nearest approach that the human mind has come to understand what life is, is that it is of the nature of fire. Wherever there is life there is heat. There are said to be in the water what we call cold-blooded animals, yet we have many reasons to believe that even in them the blood-centers have heat. The main part in creative action is carried on by the principle of fire. Fire is the animating principle in all things. Why does a piece of wood burn? First we start a fire, and it burns. We see the flame emanations, and it works of its own accord until the matter is consumed. We have given the ascendency to the fire-principle, by either friction or chemical methods, and, as soon as the equilibrium is broken, the fire-principle holds its dominancy, and consumes the material within its reach.

We are told by natural philosophers that fire is motion; that the heated molecules in a piece of iron will revolve and continue to revolve, making larger and yet larger circuits in their orbit, until finally the iron itself is dissolved by the transmutative force, and goes off in the form of gas.

There are many evidences that this principle of fire is the underlying potency in all Nature. We see worlds revolving around their central blazing sun, subject to the changeful conditions of heat and cold, each globe being filled with fire. Fire is the true, divine essence of being laid hold upon by the first principle of force, concentrated, bound, and stopped in its motion. The centrifugal, expansive fire-principle struggles against limitation; it goes out seeking liberty. It is the symbol of the infinite Being, — spirit, insphered in bondage; for all organized bodies, no matter what their forms are, have this first primitive force, bound, insphered, and caused to serve according to the needs of the structure.

Transmutation is that principle which enables us to progress, to unfold; and here again we find the same law that everywhere meets us in life, viz.: that the greatest benefactors we have we regard as our greatest adversaries. Why? Because we are naturally lazy, and hate change; the mother-principle having the dominance in us, we love the physical body and natural life, and hate that divine principle that comes in to liberate us from the old conditions, and expand our being into the higher life of the great Soul of the Universe.

66

As the physiologist looks into the structure of our bodies he finds that those little molecules that are taken in through the digestive functions are distributed throughout the system, and as soon as they, reach the embrace of life they are immediately again torn down and others put in their place. The life-essences have been made more dense, and that love of life that is concentrated within ourselves has appropriated the life of the molecule, and the husk, being unsuited for further service, is thrown off, so that all the time there is a transmutation going on. Could we but see our bodies; had we that clear eye to perceive the work that is going on in our organism; to see the flame of life luminous in us, burning like a seething furnace, and those molecules of matter whirling into that tire, coming into its embrace, and being changed there and liberated, to go to their respective uses. So, our mind is struggling constantly between these two, the principles of transmutation and cohesion. For mind is the factor of this organism, and, like the Creator, it holds sway over the subtle elements of Nature.

You cannot think of a thing, no matter what it may be, but the moment that thought enters your mind, along with it comes the sublimated essence of the thing thought of, and makes a chemical change in the molecules out of which the body is being constructed. It controls the chemist that is working deep down in the centre of the body, the Solar Plexus, the gray spot. It directs him as to what chemical essence he shall take into the body to replace that which has been taken away, and what he shall reject. Therefore, while we are in the seething furnace of life, the body, changing, being burned up and yet ever taking on more, — to preserve the balance of power between negation and positiveness, negation having the dominance, — the lower our thoughts and sympathies, the coarser our structure. Now, as we thus find this body, changing, throwing off the old, taking on the new, the mind is the master, or, as our merchants would say, the "buyer." It goes out and selects the proper elements and essences according to the uses of the occasion and surroundings and conditions that may be forced upon us. Thus in accord with what we think, we chemicalize our bodies.

Let us look into the habits of our every-day life. We take food to replenish and supply the waste, to keep up the fire and the work going on. That function of the body, "the gray-spot," that controls the stomach, is the chemist, and has control of all the chemical qualities of the body. He is most diligently and faithfully at work. He receives every telegraphic message coming from without to the brain; it is instantly transmitted to him to supply the material to form the thought, whatever the subject may be. For every thought partakes of a peculiar chemical essence that would create a like form in Nature; in other words, as the ancient alchemists tell us, every little plant is a thought-formation. Yes, it has a certain form and color, and thus expresses its quality by virtue of its own inherent chemical essence. This essence, and the sublimated essence thrown off by the creative mind, are identical; that plant was once a thought. The thought that emanates from your mind may become a plant, and a plant may become a thought of yours. Quality always expresses itself in its form.

Botanists of a truly scientific mind, when they take a leaf or plant, are certain as to what chemical properties it possesses; they can tell you all about it, because of its exact form in accordance with the law of order, so exquisitely minute in Nature. The same law obtains in your thought-life. You think a thing in your brain; that thought is telegraphed to the chemist in your body. If, during the time of eating, and for an hour after, while the chemist is doing his work of digestion, you begin to think of some unpleasant thing, this divine chemist at once begins to take into the body those exciting essences that are like that thought, and begins to build up in the body the very substance of it. Thereby the same thought will repeat itself afterwards, and rush in upon your mind with great energy. For instance, a man thinks he has a cancer. It at once is telegraphed to the chemist that there is a cancerous condition needing substance; and he at once begins to take into the body the very poisonous essences needed to supply the work of a cancer. The one thing to do is to control our thoughts by the effort of will. We must think, especially during the time the chemist is doing his work, just such thoughts as we want our body to be made up of, as we want our after-life to lie. If we do so, we shall find that this places our physical bodies, so hard to master, under our control. Thus, this control begins in the mind; all chemical action for the health or disease of your body begins in your thought. Therefore, begin with mastering your thoughts. Think what you will to think, not be driven, like an unthinking horse, hither and thither. We talk to people about controlling the mind, holding still and thinking on one subject for a few moments. They say, " I cannot think on any subject for two minutes." Why? Because they have never decided with a, will to take control of themselves, and are just like a leaf in the wind, and every influence that meets them takes control of them for the instant.

The work of thinking is the work of combustion in the body. It is fire, it is the liberation of the divine elements, by transmuting the grosser into the finer, sublimating them into a subtle element we cannot see or feel but by the aid of the unfolded finer senses. But, if we give the ascendency to the next lower principle, fermentation, whose office it is to tear down and build other organisms out of the material substances of the parent organism, then we are subject to the mind that controls the lower nature, the animal generative functions, " the Serpent." This principle takes your life-essences and forms other organisms in your children, and your lifetime is spent to bring into existence offspring. But the result is that the parent organism returns to its earth without having made much progress. If, on the contrary, you give the control to the sixth principle, transmutation, these elements, sublimated by the "fire," are drawn up to the brain, and turn all their power in that direction. These higher thoughts, telegraphed to the chemist, will cause him to take purer elements into the body, so that the whole being will be constantly getting finer and more spiritual; and, in consequence, the brain will again receive higher and yet higher thoughts, until man is enabled to think like his lather, God.

The great chemist of Nature is most abundant in his work, he gives the body any amount of fuel to work on. The only thing for us to do is to utilize it wisely, for the lower forces will certainly utilize it if we do not. If we are like the leaf in the wind, driven by our animal conditions, then this divine chemist can do nothing more than venerate life-germs and give them into the hands of "the Serpent" — the god of generation. The choice is given into our hands. If we keep the divine principle of fire, this transmuting life-energy, ever active in ourselves, then our body will be vivacious, — full of energy and animation, — our cheeks flushed, our eyes bright. And, in the midst of that blazing energy, we step out and, as we started out in our first lecture, take the name of God, "I will be what I will to be," and in the dignity of our manhood say, " I will no longer be controlled by these lower principles from whence I sprang, but I will take control of my thinking powers, and of all the seven creative forces operative in my body. I will make my body God's temple, — an instrument that will enable me to be a man; yea, more than a man, a god-man!" For the tire-principle, the very essence of the God of the universe, is in everything. why, everything we touch is filled with that divine fire! You have powers within you to begin at the right place and take control of that fire, which will immediately begin to sublimate your nature.

The flame of the little match I held before you was red; it was not clear, pure white, like the electric spark, simply because in that flame there was a great quantity of grosser elements not transmuted. Sufficient heat could be applied to that burning wood to have made the flame pure and white. "We are told that Moses saw a bush burning and it was not consumed; and he turned aside to see the wonder. He saw the fire concentrated there, but no consumption. "We are told that in combustion the particles, being liberated, revolve with great rapidity among themselves. But the finer essences of the divine being are pure; there are no crude substances at all to be taken hold of and to be transmuted. There is no grinding process to tear down the particles, and thereby to create this lurid condition; and when the fire is free from all organic life and free from negation, it consumes nothing; it is pure, calm, gentle. It is the only thing in the universe that is still: being pure, it has nothing to evolve or revolve.

At this place I wish to give you my thought about sight. "What is this sight? We look at that gas flame and from it emanates something that enables us to see all in the room. "We all know the theory of the eye: of its being a lens; of the image being thrown back on the nerves, and of the sensation produced by the waves of light telegraphed to the brain. If we examine a nerve we find it is filled with a crystal water bright and clear as the clearest spring-water. Touch that little nerve, and oh, how sensitive it is! Touch the central tube where that water is and the sense is more acute there than anywhere else. The fact is that the crystal water is the sense-element which, when brought into combustion, being so pure, so near the point of evaporation, produces no flame affecting the fibers of the nerve or its surroundings. The nerve-fluid has in itself the very quintessence of life, and therefore, of sense; one more stage of transmutation would make of it light. This the tire in the brain does; so that thought-forms appear luminous to the clairvoyant. Positive life tills the eye. Like is positive to like. Life takes cognizance of that like itself, and if the life that fills the eye is pure, and no gross substance in it at all, it will be pure, white light, and not see cross matter, but thought-essence. The fluid that fills the nerve cognizes that like itself, light cognizes light; darkness cognizes darkness. We return now to our main subject.

The principle of fermentation in our body has its centre in the generative function. It is ever tearing down the body, and giving opportunity for that life in the torn-down elements to form another organism, — a germ. Now, what should be done with this germ?

I am sorry that so many of our physiologists, so called, tell you it is necessary to give the germs to the Serpent to waste. Never was a worse lie told by a human being, — a lie that has dragged down more men and women, and ruined our domestic happiness, more than any other. If, instead of wasting that germ, you retain it in the body, the tire will take those little serpent-like formations and burn them up. It will transmit their essences to these pure elements of nerve fluid, which is life itself. The body will distribute them through every part, so that every movement will be a pleasure, and the soul will be made conscious of having a power superior to the ordinary environments. Those essences will be to us the " Substance " referred to by Paul when he said, "Faith is the substance of things." Jesus said: "If you have Faith as a grain of mustard-seed, you could say to that tree, "Be thou plucked up and cast into the sea," and it would obey you. This is the process by which to obtain Magic Power. "What a contrast between this pleasure and that which is produced while the life is being concentrated in the sex-function and thrown off in that relation! As long as you give that divine essence, created by the God within you. to the Serpent to waste and destroy, you go through life burdened, heavy, and sad. Well has such a life been called, "a long-drawn sigh"! Here are the two ways. One is following down the chain of animal life, the other is going up the ladder toward the divine Cause. There fire is our friend, burning and transmuting our body. When this is done, we have said to Force: " You shall no longer bind my elements in this narrow sphere. I will call for that divine essence of fire, and burn it out." To Discrimination we say: " You are to make my being superior to all other beings. And lo! all life is God, and everything that is is filled with that essence, and I will open out and aspire of that essence." We say to Order: "You are my servant, and shall create for me thought-formations according to that higher principle. You shall build for me my heaven." For all the heaven we shall ever have is the thoughts we are thinking; they will be our future consciousness; out of your thoughts you are building your heaven or your hell. We shall say to Cohesion: "You shall be my Strength of Will, conserve and maintain my body and furnish the appropriate elements for my laboratory so that I shall have abundance of all I need." We shall say to Fermentation: " You also are my servant, and through your subtle power (usually known as Psychic Power), I will send forth my thought to do service in whatever department of Nature I will." We shall say to Transmutation: "You shall transmute the gross elements of my body into those most subtle, that I may be superior to earth, and belike my Maker, and through you I will say to Sensation: You shall be my messenger to keep me informed of all I wish to know of this world and its laws and methods, and shall make me conscious of the thoughts of men, angels, and of God, and cause me to live in the enjoyment of the Paradise of God's Thought forever."

For, as that Love-nature gathers and provides the necessary elements out of which I make and transmute this divine essence of being, and make of it whatever I will to make, Nature thus becomes subject to my will, because I control the Thinking Power by the Will. By taking the Name of the Creator, that implies "the will to be what I will to be." These powers are in you, and all there is for you to do is to take hold of one thing at a time. Yes, take hold of your own body first; be master of your own mind, then be master of your own senses, and then you can easily be master of all the other forces, and fire will be found to possess a consciousness that our thought will control in all its forms until in all its phases it will become obedient to your thought and your will.

When the essences of our being are so sublimated fire is held in abeyance within ourselves, and if you have taken control of that fifth principle, and utilized the sixth, you will find the truth of the stories that come to us across the water from the Orient of persons who, through these processes, have conserved a natural fire in their own bodies capable of kindling a real fire by blowing their breath upon ordinary fuel. But if you allow the Serpent to waste and destroy the finer substances of your nature, that seething fire burning within you will become a smoldering mass of ruins, so closed with gross material that it cannot be luminous and bright; whereas, if you turn it in the other direction, you will clear up the body, fill it with that crystal element, and the fire will burn bright like the electric spark, and be the light of Life, Knowledge, Wisdom, Power like unto the great Cause and Source from which it comes. All things, both earthly and invisible, will begin to be your servants; for the earthly things are only the expression of the invisible things, through the action of the principles I have shown you.

Such powers are in your bodies, and if you stop and think as you should, going through this course of lessons, you will know just where to begin and what to do, and how to conserve these forces, making them your servants. And, when you have done so, you come to this first and last principle, the seventh stage of unfoldment which we are to consider, when fire will have become your servant and you the master.

The ancients had in their thought the same work of sublimating the essences, and subjecting the seven forces, and came to a point in their unfoldment, when their inner consciousness was illuminated, and told us there was a place where there was nothing but that pure, perfect, white light, the most sacred place in the universe, — the home of God. At Niagara Falls, this winter, as I was standing and looking at the tremendous fall of water, my soul seemed to be opened, and I was conscious of that great centre of pure whiteness; it was to me a conscious vision as of a place; yet I am not prepared to say it is a locality. Let it be what it will, that pure ethereal whiteness brings a calm of restful satisfaction.

We talk about pleasure and enjoyment. "We know nothing about it. Not one of us has anything like an adequate idea of it, and we never can have until the old Serpent is absolutely enslaved to our will. "When this is done, and the inner consciousness, that most beautiful and sublime life, has come to be unfolded within, and we have a cognizance of that eternal rest and satisfaction, realizing that it permeates our inner being, then there will be a realization that you have attained a point where there is an absolute consciousness that if this body should pass away, should be consumed in the flames, you would be unmoved, your soul satisfied, restful, and at peace, consciousness going on and on into the unbounded realms of knowledge, wisdom, enjoyment, surpassing all the thought of sense. This consciousness may and yet will be ours.

I am not endeavoring to get you to believe any doctrine. I come to you as men and women, able to think; and I ask you to think, not for my sake, but for your own, for humanity's sake; to turn your thoughts in the right directions; to rise above that dark and dismal sphere of a mere animal life. Be men, and come into the divine inheritance, and " be what you will to be," having passed through Transmutation, to awake in everlasting "Glory."

72

יהוה

"I will be what I will to be."

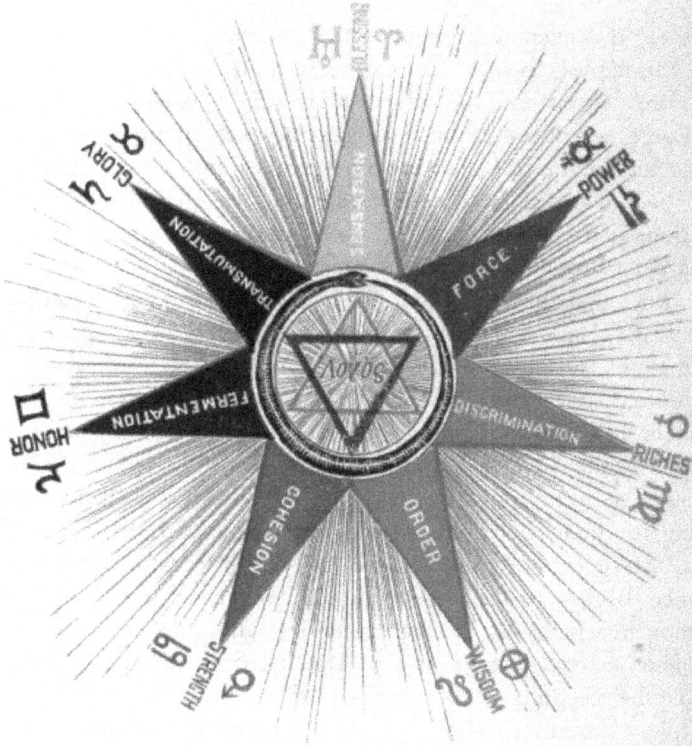

73

EIGHTH LECTURE. SENSATION.

THE SEVENTH OF THE SEVEN CREATIVE PRINCIPLES.

We are this evening brought to the consideration of the seventh of the seven principles, being the one denominated on the diagram as " Sensation." To enforce the subject more fully I would say, that, beginning with Force, we traced around, considering each of the seven principles in their order. Each is united to the other, and cannot work without that unity; but, as we go on, each successive one is more and yet more potent in its operation, as it calls into unity all the forces that have preceded it; so that, having been brought, this evening, to the seventh, it necessitates the other six in order that this may exist. We begin with Force as the principle that concentrates and brings matter into existence. The second principle discriminates and polarizes the atoms of matter. The third gives order to all formation. The fourth causes all thing's, after the formation has taken place, to cohere and adhere together, and makes growth of vegetation possible. The fifth is the state of fermentation, wherein the elements of which the vegetable is composed are changing, the life-forces concentrating and forming for themselves independent organisms wherein to manifest their nature, the first mode of which life is, through transmutation, when insect existence begins to take nourishment, which is transmuted from the condition in which it is in when taken into the little organism, to that like the higher essences of its nature. The result of this combination makes possible the reception of the principle of sensation.

While, in itself, sensation is a distinct principle, yet, without its alliance to matter, to organism, there is no sensation. Sensation is a mode of consciousness. I presume that there is no word more commonly used, and none having so little known of its nature and quality as the principle of sensation. In fact, the real principles underlying it can never be comprehended by human intelligence; but it may be apprehended. We may, this evening, be enabled to trace its workings, to observe the laws and methods and localities; but when we have asked the question, What is sensation? we can only answer, that sensation is the instrument or the mode by which the life reaches out and preserves itself, the mode of cognizance, the instrumentality by which knowledge comes to life. Then, when we have come to consider the idea of sensation from this interior standpoint, we ask the question again, What is life? Here we are lost in the infinite ocean of Cause, — the great source of being, the spirit essence which alone has the power of cognizance.

The interior essence of being has, in all organisms, formed instruments for itself by which it reaches out and comes in contact with the physical

74

world, through which contact it takes cognizance of it. This principle of sensation becomes the means by which the life is preserved from destruction, by itself or by its enemies. Sensation is the germ of all thought, from which all thought originates. Were it not for sensation thought would not be known in the world.

Thought has unfolded from sensation in this way: Those insect existences grow and develop and increase, feed one upon another, multiplying qualities, and thus necessitating additional functions, and also organs, until higher and yet higher stages of insect existence appear in the world. Sensation lies at the foundation of the multiplicity of organic life. The sense of sight, the sense by which we cognize light, is the means by which the eye has been formed. The sense of pain and pleasure, or the idea of being hurt, and the effort to preserve themselves from destruction among their fellows, has caused them to earnestly desire. Again a thought has been created which answers to that desire, to be able to take cognizance of, and protect themselves from the adversaries of their life. This effort to take cognizance we see in the little insects that have no eyes, but shoot out a feeler and feel their way around them. They are standing quietly, or may be moving along rapidly, and a little unusual noise or sound will cause them to stop suddenly, and their little feelers will go out in every direction, and, as soon as they are made conscious of some unusual fellow-creature, of whatever size or character it may be, they at once seek their methods of self-protection. Here it is that the necessity of throwing the senses into the extremities springs up.

As we come to examine and look after the elements, or substances, if you please, in which the sense is found most dominant, we find it is in that crystal water that is usually denominated, "nerve fluid," and with which the nerve is filled. In it is the most acute sense, and wherever the thought goes, there goes its essence of life with it. The blind man I referred to before, who has been taught to read with the finders, soon gets so that he can read with astonishing rapidity; scarcely is it necessary for him to touch the raised letters. I knew a man that was totally blind, yet, if a cat ran across the street before him he knew it. He had been in the habit of throwing the senses to the front, and that habit had made the nerve-centers so acute that they took cognizance of a shadow or of anything that passed before them.

"We are taught by the masters of the Orient, both ancient and modern, that we should conquer sensation. What does this imply? "We conquer that which gives rise to thought. Yes, we conquer this basis, this foundation principle, and we turn our attention toward the cause; that is, after the work of evolution has gone to its limit in ourselves, then we no longer feel as though we were down here on the earth, but draw our consciousness, our cognizance, from the earth condition, as we see the butterfly arising from a lower form. Having developed the interior and spiritual essences, and filled the body with their purer essence of life, through a persistent conserving of the life-potencies within the body; having conquered all the baser nature, the principle of uncontrolled generation; having turned all the forces into the higher uses of the body, and filled it with luminous life-elements, — then the body begins to be able to take cognizance of purer, higher, and grander thought than can be found upon the earth-plane; for, when we begin to conquer the sensations that come to us from the physical body, we at once reach out and begin to sense the more subtle and more perfect thought-emanations of the Creator. There can be no effort made without a desire. Desire is the method of prayer, as has been well said. " Prayer is the sincere desire of the heart." Love is a form of desire. God is love.

In the consideration of these seven principles Cohesion was shown to be the mother-nature, the mother-love being the active one in the world, that we admire and respect more than all others as the preserver of all things, as that principle that has such zealous care over all its subjects. When the mother-nature is well embodied, and has its full and comprehensive understanding in us, and we come to recognize the subject that we have been talking to you about, namely, that we are only one of a great family of the Infinite Father, God, and that all men, all creatures, all life, all formation are alike the offspring of the one great Mind, then we enlarge the sphere of the mother-love from merely that narrow family relation, to become like the Divine Mother that loves all her creatures alike, that is no respecter of persons. The pure mother would give her life, would work until the flesh was worn from her bones, would lie down at night exhausted, sleepless, and anxious for the sake of providing for her offspring, for her children, for their education, for their qualification to enable them to step out on the field of action to take care of themselves in the world.

When that mother-love in us has had its perfect unfoldment, and we look out upon the world of humanity and see that all are God's children, — and we are the sons of God, — that we are joint-heirs, and, therefore, these are all our children, then we enlarge the sphere, and take into the encompassing love all things, and we labor with diligence, combined with divine wisdom, that we may educate and uplift and relieve the suffering of all God's creatures. This desire, when formulated, will at once possess and polarize our inner consciousness, so that it will reach out and begin to take cognizance of the Everlasting Father, and then, and not until then, comes to us, ever, the prayer — The Lord's Prayer — that we have so frequently heard in our churches, where Jesus says, "In this manner pray ye." The very first utterance is " Our Father." Now, we are told by the same authority, " Without faith is sin." And without a consciousness of that object to which we speak there can be no faith, there can be no adequate concentration. How can you concentrate the mind, the desire, upon an object, upon a principle, upon a spirit, unless there is some means within you by which you may take cognizance of that something to which you are reaching out in love? Can you love something that you know nothing of; that you have no idea of? No. Go to those devotional ones and ask them, Do you love God? Oh, yes, they answer. What is your idea of God, we then ask? Can we get them to define it at all? Do they not usually refuse, because their own reason condemns it? Yet, when they will define it, what is the result? They have pictured to themselves a grand man, a high, ideal man, and that man is the image of their worship. In that sense they may be elevated by having fixed a standard of manhood, desiring that standard, reaching out toward it, inspiring from it. It has been a means of the elevation of the race for ages past. But yet it is not the highest one. While men have been in this state, and have pictured for themselves a man, and have reached out in their aspirations toward that man, though there may have come thoughts directly from the true God of the Universe, they have been reaching out to something like themselves, — reaching out merely through the external senses.

I want here to call your attention to a thought. Every thought that you think must of necessity have a form. You cannot think anything without putting it into form. We will illustrate it thus: The spiritual man dwells within. Now, if a thought comes to a man from without, reaches the senses without, and, through the senses, becomes conscious to the spiritual entity within, then it must give the exact inversion of the form that it was in when it left the thinker's mind. In other words, the type that makes the impression has the wrong side up. It is inverted.

In the same way the human intelligence has received every thought of God inverted. It is a wonderful thing, if you will stop and think of it, to take the thoughts, the doctrines, that are received by the thinking world at large. "We have received them through this; living in the five senses. How thoroughly they have inverted every divine thought, — even the one I have just called your attention to, the Lord's Prayer! Where is there a Christian on the continent to-day who, when he prays, " Father, let thy kingdom come, and thy will be done on earth, as it is done in heaven," if you should say, "Stop! what do you mean, — to desire that God's will should be done here on the earth as it is in heaven? " He does not expect that, but means all the time the other way about. " Let me go up there and do thy will in heaven, for I cannot down hero on earth." Just inverted. Go through the entire revelation of the Scriptures, and you find that the mind of men who have come to these things from the external senses and reasoning of the brain, exclusively from the external senses, has every idea exactly inverted; therefore the five senses cannot be trusted for spiritual discernment. You cannot trust them any more than you can read the type before the impression is made. What must be done? The inner consciousness must be opened to the Soul of the Universe. There must be a development from within, so that the soul itself, the inmate that dwells within the house, has a power independent of the five senses, to go out into the cause-world, and to receive into the innermost consciousness the thought of God, and project it out to the world. We have to go by ourselves, independent of any man, of any teachers, and reach out for the knowledge by that innermost principle of love which is God-love, and there is no God-love but that which is love to all his creatures. And if I love my wife, my children, my own little circle, to the exclusion of all others, and even perchance to the oppression of others, — which we see all the time, — this is self-love, and not God-love.

Now, this principle of true love is as necessary and, in fact, it is (lie necessary principle to have always active, being the true sense, the soul-sense, which can be opened and made a receptacle of the thoughts of God, that work from the interior out through the exterior. " We must grow," says the Hondo master, " as the flower grows; " and the flower gathers its vitality from within, and unfolds from within to without, and the external is being constantly thrown off. Thus we must grow from within. We must cultivate the interior senses to the suppression and perfection of the external senses.

There is nothing more deceptive to the world than the senses, in more ways than the inspirational. The sense of pleasure is the most deceptive thing that we have. Pleasure is nothing more than life in motion. There can be no sensation without something that produces a movement of the life elements. There must be a cause of motion before there can be any sensation. Even for the sensation that belongs to the interior and spiritual there must be a spiritual cause to produce it before it can be manifest. We sense the touch of some person or thing. There has been a movement from without that has caused the sensation.

If we trace further, and ask the question, "What is that we call pleasure? " we feel all animated and joyous, and the bright red blood springs to the cheeks. The eyes glow with all the luster, and fullness, and vitality that fills the body; we are animated, we are happy; but that lasts for a little time only, and we begin to feel tired. Now what has taken place? This life, and animation, and joy, was merely a going out and throwing off of the finest elements of our life. A waste. Yes, perhaps a waste of the purest elements that we possess. That is all there is in it. We we re simply using and exhausting the very essences of being, and it was pleasure while it was going on, but the reaction comes afterwards. The very principle that controls the animal world in the function of generation is sensation; the sensation of all kinds of pleasure rules sufficiently strong to dominate Over all mankind as an incentive to action; and why? Because the very finest essences of our existence are being concentrated and formulated in a germ, using the divinest principle of our being, and in that action of concentration all these finer essences in their action impart a sense of pleasure. And the final exodus of that essence is the ultimate of that pleasure. Then come exhaustion and repulsion. The body is weakened; the mind is lost; the vitalizing principle that animates the molecules of the body has gone. Right here can be found the cause of our being so subject to diseased conditions. The mind may be very active, the brain fully engaged in some useful, and perhaps thoughtful labor. Finally the body gets full of life and animation. Every molecule seems to be aglow with life. We perhaps overfeed the body to secure .additional strength, or as a matter of habit. Finally, when the body is filled with this additional material, there comes the demand of the lower, the sense-nature; it reaches the mind; that life-essence is then concentrated in the sex-nature and goes out from us. The body is exhausted. The creative part of this animating, vivifying life that permeated all the particles of the body is gone. Death has entered the body. Millions of molecules of matter are left without their animating essence. At once the divine mother-nature, co-working with the wonderful mechanic, order, concentrates her forces upon the most fit, leaving all the rest to be thrown off, and the work begins in the body to gather up these dead atoms and bring them into the blood, and carry them off through the ordinary channels of effete matter. In that coalition we feel tired, languid, irritable. We are angry at the least thing. We do not know why. But stop and think, and we will find that there is an interior will that is called into action. Every nerve is strained. All the forces are diligently at work in the body to cleanse it from these dead carcasses that are left there because of the injudicious waste of the finer essences of the system. Perhaps they are resurrected in another form. But our life must now be taxed. We must go to work and tear down and get rid of those dead and impure molecules in the body, and the act of doing so taxes the body to its utmost. Supposing, at that time, some poisonous condition comes in, — some extra taxation on the body from another source, — the body is then like an army that has an adversary to fight hand to hand, man to man; and now the enemy is suddenly reinforced, and you fall victims, simply because you have not maintained that perfect equilibrium of life.

We are taught by the masters that we must obtain that deep soul-calm that is unmoved under all circumstances; that we must move through the world as one with power to be and to do what he wills to be and to do. Such is necessary. No one will be master until he can move through this world having sufficient mastery to be unmoved, self-controlled. "We would not think a man was very much of a master of his enemies, if, when he walked through their midst, he went skulking here and there. He is the master who walks through the midst of his enemies without fear, without a tremor, feeling within himself that he is master of his surroundings; moving with a calm self-possession.

We must conquer our senses; for they exhaust the vital fluids and leave us depleted, and, whilst we are ruled by them, we are jostled here and there. We are crowded by adversaries from within and without, and these adversaries without, and the irregularity of our own life within, keep us continually in this struggling condition. Here poising your mind on one object, dwelling there day after day, and week after week, will not give you the needed power; no ordinary drill will suffice; this power must come from within, — from the forces that you possess, from the actions and laws of your being.

That which allies us to this world is sensation. It was there our consciousness began. We seek its cause; we know its workings; we know what is accomplished when sensations are active within us. Therefore, we watch them as we would watch a thief. When we feel that sensation is in the body, we know there is some cause for it. Watch carefully what is being done; what is being accomplished. Watch from the inner consciousness; hold still all other senses; look into the mind, and observe the springs of thought and sensation. Be quiet. Listen with the stillness of every function and faculty of the mind and body; and, as you listen and question, — for the God that dwells within you is identical with the God that rules the universe, both in power and wisdom, — that God within you is able to answer every question. Listen to his voice!

No wonder, as Isaiah said, " When I spake, there was none to answer. When I called there was none to say, 'Here am I.'" Because, as the voice of God calling in the garden (Whose garden? Why, the garden of your God!"), when all these animal senses are active, he speaks, and speaks, and speaks again, and there is no ear to hear. We are too busy with these inverted senses. The glitter and glamour of a world of sense stultifies the mind, deafens the ear; and, though it calls aloud, we think it is the voice of fancy, and again we go more and more deeply into the senses. The teachers of spiritual laws tell us we must be careful and not run after phantoms; that God is spirit, yet God never any more approaches man; that man is isolated from God. Oh, sad condition if it were so! No! God dwells within the soul, is enthroned upon the will, rules in the life-forces, serves as a faithful and over-indulgent mother, anxious for the good of all; serving and sustaining you ever, though you do evil; constantly laboring to preserve your life. If you waste the gold of pure life he at once goes to work diligently to replace it. On and on the divine principle labors, until, finally, you have sinned "against the day of grace; " in other words, you have so exhausted the body that it has become unfit for other uses, and that same principle disintegrates the body for service in other directions.

Then the sense that we want is that inner sense that listens, hears, feels, and cognizes God, the Cause, the indwelling pure Spirit; and, to do so, the man who is master of himself, has reason above sensation, he knows the voice of the Almighty as it calls within him. God acts and speaks through the consciousness, is zealous, in the man or the woman, for the good of all men and all women. This should cause you and me to desire, with the same earnest, anxious love that the mother has for her child, to labor for humanity, to desire their well-being, to desire that they should come into this divine consciousness.

"When heavenly desire is active, then man can pray; but not without it can he pray effectually. Then the prayer of that soul that looks out upon the human family and the world, and sees the fallen condition we are in to-day, and reaches out with that pure thought that they should have: " Oh, for wisdom and power! that I might work under thy divine guidance for the elevation of my brethren, of those under my care! — Oh, that I might become an instrument in the hands of that Infinite Power to work that I may alleviate, elevate, and strengthen; that I may bring my fellows into the consciousness of that glorified life! "

We are now like the tube that has been lying across the rapid rushing stream until its interior is tilled with gravel and clay and dirt; but, if it is turned around lengthwise with the stream, the waters rush through and clean it, and the waters have free course through it. So you and I. When our interior is turned in a direct line to the Great Soul that loves the world and gives itself for its elevation, when we are thus blessed with the divine life, the current flows through us as the mighty rushing river flows through the tube to all the creatures for whom we desire this " Blessing " that we have obtained.

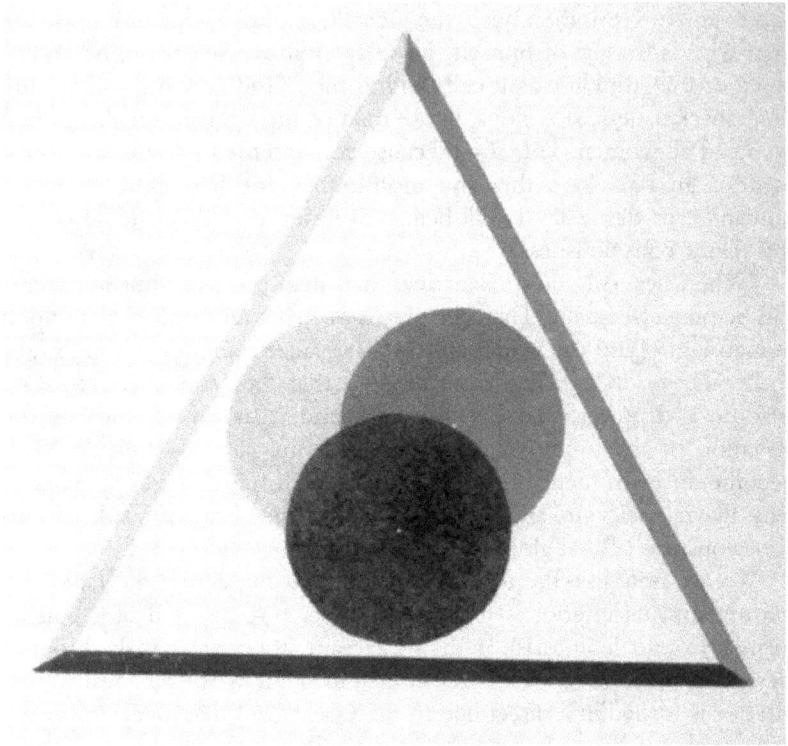

NINTH LECTURE. COLORS.

We will accept that there are but three primary colors, and that from these three all colors may he made. It is also accepted that there are but three primary principles in Nature.

This primary condition or manifest principle in man is represented by the triangle. Red is the base of the material flesh. It is the color of the blood, or animal life, the force principle, or the first principle of Nature, the primary that calls together and binds and enspheres all things. It is that color which gives to the sense the inclination to self-preservation; which inclination, when carried into the intellectual realm of humanity, is selfishness. (Of course, the more intellectual the persons who indulge in selfishness may be, the greater ability they will have to make that selfish principle one of great evil and oppression.)

I take up the subject of colors mainly for this reason: There are thousands to-day whose sixth sense is being opened, so that they begin to have a conscious perception of thought-forms, of spirit entities, as they are called, and actually are, in some cases; and the sixth sense is one that ramifies in such a multifarious manner that it would take a whole evening's consideration to even present to you anything like an adequate idea of its extent.

As we begin at the lowest sense and come up to the highest, we find in their order that they expand in their utility and power. So, when we take another step beyond the five senses into the realm of cause, or rather make a nearer approach to cause, with this sixth sense, which reaches out more largely and broadly into that realm, and in many cases, in my own experience especially, with those persons whose minds are allied principally to sight, as the sixth sense, or, as some have called it, " the spirit eyes " are opened, first begin to see a variety of colors. Therefore, this subject of colors is in order, because of the teachings which are being given from time to time, not only here, but throughout the world wherever Theosophy has found a hearing. Those teachings, in fact, lead to the unfoldment of these higher senses that we are not now conscious of. The people that are most perfectly endowed by, or, rather, allied to, Nature in its purity, in its order and harmony, are those whose minds, when the sixth sense begins to be opened, will take cognizance of colors and forms.

Forms relate to the magnetism of the universe and the language of the Creator, because all forms are thoughts, and all thoughts are forms. Otherwise, they would never act upon our consciousness, or we would never be conscious of them. Therefore, when the " spirit eyes," or the sixth sense is opened, colors and forms present themselves before the vision. These are the thoughts we find employed throughout the Hebrew prophecies. "We find that the imagery, which was the language of creation, of beasts of varied characters, birds, creeping things, all varieties of animate and vegetable existence, was called into use to illustrate or express the " word " or thought of the Creator.

Thought imaged itself upon the mind of the prophets of antiquity, and we are not far remote in our natures from those old seers and sages. The thing for us to do is to live in accordance with the same methods with which they lived, and the same powers are ours. I do not think that the race has declined, or that the interior powers, which we once possessed, from eighteen hundred to six thousand years ago, have passed away by means of diminution or loss. God's laws never change. They are the same forever; and though, through foolish teachings, we may have believed that these interior powers belonged only to a special few; though we may have formed the idea of a god-man, or a man-god, who controlled his subjects, as do kings of the lower plane of existence, by edicts, and by being angry or pleased; and though we may have thought that the people at one period of the world were favored by this superior monarch, and that this favor has now been withdrawn, yet we should be sorry to believe this now. "We believe that grand old book itself which tells us, from the beginning of Genesis to the end of Revelation, that the God, of whose thought it is the record never changes, works always by law and according to law, and that it is we who change. By virtue of these changes we are either come into more perfect harmony with his law, and become more cognizant of its workings, or into less harmony, and become less cognizant of its workings or of any higher principles of Nature.

The first color, then, that relates directly to the human organism, to the animal forces, is the color red. This has in it the property of heat, because its function is concentrativeness. It is magnetic to the extreme; and, because it is magnetic and concentrative, it is heating.

The second color is that outgrowth of the workings of the spirit upon the physical body, representing the mind and the first principles of mind, which is order, and is symbolized by the color blue, which is the counterpart of green, the symbol of mother Nature.

The third color, that of sensation, is yellow. That is the color of sense. It represents in its character rest, harmony; rest, simply because sensation belongs to knowledge, and is of that golden perfection of spirit-life. The yellow represents, therefore, perfection. The shade of color always has its own significance, which we will consider hereafter. These are the three primary or foundation principles that underlie all others.

The sun's spectrum, having the seven color-rays clearly defined, is representative of seven distinctly different principles. It is unquestionably a fact in Nature that there are seven distinct color-rays, as there are seven notes in music, seven sounds of harmony.

The seven qualities or primary creative energies that we have been talking about as principles are found in each and every one of us. As is shown in our new system of " Solar Biology," these seven are seven vitals or primaries. There are, in all, twelve spheres of uses or organic qualities in man; but the seven are the vital principles, without which man cannot exist. These seven, as they are known in music, in simple music demonstrated as a fact, have several octaves one above another, their vibrations differing one from the other. There are vibrations so rapid and others so slow so as to produce no discernible sound to the ordinary senses.

The time will come when we can distinguish sounds by their colors. In fact, we read that there are those who see, in every note of music, the color. Not only the color, but when these notes are interblended according to the law of order (which order is characteristic in the human mind, and music produces a harmony corresponding), there are those who see animate forms springing forth from the key-board, like living, active, spiritual beings. Why? Because these seven creative principles, no matter how they are expressed, or how they are called into action, act under the same great law of the primal creative thought, the purpose of which was a harmonic Man.

"We identify red with force, the animal principle in Nature. It is the lowest of all the colors. If you would sit in this room when the evening shades are coming on, and look at these colors on the star you would find that the yellow would disappear first. The order of their disappearance would be such that the red would be the last one to disappear in the darkness. It would become black, and would stand out before your eyes as if that were the only color on that chart; and that color would appear black, being the strongest of all the colors.

Pink we consider one of the seven. The idea embodied in that delicate tint is love. It is a combination and interblending of the red and the white; so that there arises a beautiful tint of the living, active, vital principle expressing purity of character. When there is white and enough of the red, there comes to be a manifestation of discrimination. It also expresses thought, repulsion at the least coarseness, grossness, or impurity in Nature. When we see the pink flower growing, notice the feeling which it produces in the mind, especially in those who have any susceptibility for the line arts. How delicate it appears! We feel as if we were almost too coarse to touch that beautiful, delicate little blossom. It appears delicate, as this color is the discriminative, the pure element, and produces purity of feeling in all conditions. It is the principle that should be the one cultivated by all means more than all others, by those who are studying to unfold and perfect their own lives. What we want is purity of life, and by purity of life we obtain the purest mind-potencies. We should therefore desire purity.

So, when your minds began to take cognizance of that beyond the five senses, and you see before your inner eyes this delicate tint of pink, you may know that you have succeeded thus far to attract to yourselves the influence that will work its beautiful work in you, will separate you from all inversions, all impurity, all misuse, and will lead your mind into the pure and the good.

The third principle, the principle order, is blue. We look up into the sky, and above us is that beautiful blue. Why? There everything works in exactly the order in which the Infinite Mind has placed it. There is nothing out of order there. No jostling together of worlds, no confusion. All is perfect order, and it is a perfect blue. Those of you who heard the discourse on order can readily apply the law, this evening, to the color blue.

The antithesis, the opposition of order in Nature, is represented by the color gray, indigo mixed with red. It is the combination existing in matter when order is being misplaced, confusion is being created. The law of order is being taken away from the chemical or vegetable substances. They are being decomposed. The indigo being the most powerful decomposing ray, the red being the most powerful concentrative ray, the two struggle together in their work of tearing down the old, whilst the red holds tenaciously to the life-essences that are in the plant so that they may be formed into another organism. For the law of God in the workings of these seven principles allows nothing to be wasted. There is no such thing as retrogression in the divine law. Nothing in the world can retrograde in the absolute sense. Of course, man may be said to retrograde as a man, as an individual, as a personality, or a conscious ego; but, as to the essences of his being, there is no retrogression. As soon as retrogression

begins in a person the divine law of fermentation comes in and begins to tear the man to pieces, to scatter his parts, and he begins to die. He may, of course, attract to himself and embody in himself a greater amount of the first principle, and thus be a strong animal; but as a strong animal he has to serve, so that there is no absolute retrogression after all. Indeed there cannot be. This principle of the red is struggling with the indigo in the plant to maintain the vital principles and to see to it that there is no retrogression in Nature. It lays hold of the life-essences of the plant, and organizes an insect existence which fills the air with winged insects. Millions crawl and fly in the season when vegetation decays in large quantities. Thus the principles of red and blue are overcome by that higher above them.

But cohesion, the fourth principle, green, is the potent conserver of organic life. It holds and binds together the life-essences. Vegetation takes that color because that is the principle which is most active. It is the symbol of the unfoldment of vegetable life. Therefore it expresses itself in this color, because, as we have shown you, as we advance in these seven colors higher and yet higher the immediately above contains all below. The color green, then, represents the mother-nature that preserves and holds together all things. It represents fertility; it represents growth, unfoldment. Therefore

86

it looks after the preservation of its own, and gathers, and provides for those under its care. To provide is the province of the mother-nature. Therefore growth is always expressed and symbolized in the Hebrew prophecies by the color green.

Take the twelve stones of the twelve signs of the Zodiac, and each of the twelve stones has its color. The foundation of the Temple is represented as having twelve stones, and the color of the stones is referred to in other places. "Were it not that the color was intended to express a meaning as well as the stone, the color would not have been given in addition to the name. The name would have been sufficient. The stones, as crystallizations, are the symbols of all the principles which exist. Therefore, when we see a crystallization which is red, we can say that there is a single principle crystallized there. When we see pink, we see there two principles crystallized; when we see blue, we see three crystallized principles. So in green we have four principles. Yet, in each of these combinations, that which absorbs, or the color which rules, is the one which is active. But all the others must also be there, or else no organic form would be found.

Yet another strange fact. In the most of crystallizations there will be found a definite form. Some of the most beautiful formations and colors are found in crystals. The most exquisite colors upon which the eye ever looked are to be found in them. When we understand the language of colors we will begin to understand the Bible. None of us can ever know much about the Bible until we understand all that is symbolized by this star, all that is expressed in this system of the seven creative principles. The Bible is a book of science which deals with the workings of the laws of Nature. It in no sense tells of a God who issues edicts and then changes his mind. It tells of a people, it is true, who had thoughts of that kind. Now we have come to a time when people want facts. They want laws. And when we have laws clearly defined then we will find that in that old book, the Bible, is more scientific knowledge than in any number of books which you could obtain, and this notwithstanding the great amount of error which has crept into the book, owing to its passing through the hands of a people on a low plane of unfoldment. There is no book its equal. You may go to the Vedas, the Shastras, all the sacred books and books of science, go where you will, there is none that deals so directly and so harmoniously with the central laws and methods of Nature as this book. There is none which can be compared with this for its mystic sayings. The Scripture writers' words could not be understood by the people, so they were put into similes for those who were thinkers upon the laws of Nature. They were expressed in the language of God; and the language of God is form. And, as we read the old prophets, we find, "I saw, and behold that beast had so many horns, so many eyes, and so many heads."

87

A person blind to the Esoterics of life says, " That is all nonsense." To him so it is. But to those who understand them these symbols are full of meaning. So with those of us who possess the sixth sense, the principle of clairvoyance or clear sight, those of us who are dwelling in the Esoteric; — it is no matter by what name you call us, — you are aware that we are not associated or assimilated with any sect. We are the class who want knowledge and truth. We belong to ourselves. There is no truth for us save that which belongs to the law of divine order in Nature. We want the facts of things that are, not things which appear to be and are not.

The principle of green, then, in its ultimate, being that of the mother-nature or soul-power, the feminine, the coherent principle, it follows that when it is ultimated in the feelings of manhood and womanhood, it will be an expression of the principle of strength, — strength which will enable one to accomplish anything, to do whatever one wills to do. Thus, when we see the color green in its different shades, we see symbolized to us that strength, that maintaining power by virtue of which we can go on and unfold and grow and manifest the higher and nobler qualities of our divine selfhood.

Indigo-blue represents the fifth principle and belongs to the principle of fermentation. The principle of fermentation, however, is not always seen. Indigo-blue appears usually to the mind as black, representing death. If you take the real indigo-blue you will find it would be hard to distinguish it from black. It belongs, therefore, to that condition we call death. Black, again, represents evil, the adverse principle which destroys. Blackness or darkness is a symbolic expression of the law that is brought to light by the principle of fermentation, of the serpent, the adversary, the principle of evil, the tearer down of the unfit. If I should see before me an image of blackness, and that image of blackness continued to follow me, I should at once begin to turn my eye within, for something wrong, something that I was doing, something that I was thinking, some habit of life that was wrong and was causing this image of blackness to be ever present before me. I should go right into myself, and begin to study, begin to examine, begin to think, until I found out what was wrong; and when I did, the image would go.

Blackness is used all through the Bible as symbolic of mourning and death. It belongs to the principle of destruction, the adversary, the evil thoughts which act to destroy. Black is usually found on the earth in swampy ground, where there is stagnant water, but sometimes, on looking across, the color seems to be indigo-blue. You may observe a pond of stagnant water, where fermentation has its full freedom of action. Look across the surface and you see the indigo-blue quite distinctly because there is decomposition going on. The order of prior formation is being broken up and thrown off, leaving a distinct shade of black.

The sixth principle is represented by violet. We are told, by those who have analyzed it, that this color is the most powerful chemical ray which we have. But while it is the most powerful chemical ray, how quickly it will leave us! "We have, perchance, a beautiful carpet of that exquisite color. The sun strikes it, and it disappears. It is an active principle, — the sixth, it transcends the five senses, and brings us, as a next step, to spirit, the divinest of all things of which we can take cognizance. The principle itself is not spirit, but the next step to sensation. It is the active agent. It is Gabriel, the archangel of the Divine. It is the chief actor, the chief minister in all Nature, because it produces sensation and rightly used ultimates in blessing. This delicate tint, wherever it appears, is good, very good. But remember that, regarding all things that are good, the better they are, the more closely will they be associated with those things which make the most potent factors for evil.

If in the imagining power of my brain I begin to read the language of God, and I see before me the image of a carnivorous beast, a destroyer of flesh, and I see that this beast is represented in red and in violet, I may say at once there is something determined to change my relation from this state of being to that of another. Why so? Because it has the ultimate power to change. Its function of red is force: its form is that of a destroyer. Therefore it is about to tear and destroy, and has the power with which to do it; and being associated with violet would intimate death, violet alone would imply transition to a higher state. What beautiful tints of violet we see sometimes before the mind! I presume there is hardly a person before me who does not sometimes see these colors.

We are taught by our teachers that these forms and colors are "all imagination; " and so they are, but of the kind of imagination by which God made the world. Imagination is the most potent factor in the world. There is nothing having form in the universe but is the outcome or creation of the imagination of the Infinite Mind. We will learn also enough, sometime, to know that there is nothing, it matters not whence it comes, or in what form it may be shaped, but has a definite meaning. Every image means something. There is no such thing as chance in Nature. There is a law underlying all life. So watch these imagining powers. There is not a person before me to-night who has not, at times, on going to sleep, seen colors or images before the mind.

If you want to know the condition in which you are, just concentrate your mind and see what color first appears. If you find the red coming up before you, that being the color that portrays destruction, you had better stop. Perhaps you may begin to see the beautiful color of violet, or a tinge of yellow or gold, or perhaps a bright crystal green. Beware, however, lest you be deceived by the green. There are two kinds of green; one the beautiful crystal green, and the other the dark, swampy green, the one very good, the other very bad. The one is the divine mother which comprehends all life everywhere, under all conditions. The other, the selfish mother-love that would hold and retard.

We next have the seventh principle, — sensation, represented by yellow. All through the Hebraic prophecies you will find constant reference to "gold," the pure gold, the golden this and the golden that. (I refer to the Hebrew scriptures because, as I told you before, they deal with the language of cause more than do any other books in the world.) Now why is this? Because gold expresses the nature and embodiment of the principle of yellow, or triumph, the perfection of the seven creative principles. Our Mongolian brothers understand the occult value of colors. The yellow flag is, with the Chinese, the symbol of the Divine. It is an expression of the perfection of the seven creative principles. Referring to the essences of life being conserved and regenerated, renewed and perfected in the organism of man, the principle therein is called God.

"When the principle refers to the god-life, it is symbolized in a stone, in a crystal or yellow-stone, which you will verify on looking over the list of stones in the Bible. Oh, this beautiful yellow! How quickly, on entering a room where there is a great deal of yellow in the carpet, or on the walls, with a harmonious blending of a few other colors you will feel inspired, perhaps, to say: " Oh, I experience such rest." If under excitement, you seem to rest at once.

On looking over the world to-day we see that there has never been a time in its history when humanity has been so ill at ease, so oppressed by business and the cares of life. Go through our stores to-day, and yon will find that yellow is more extensively used than ever before. In carpets, on wall-papers, in everything relating to home and surroundings, yellow is manifesting itself. And those of you who are familiar with our work, "Solar Biology," will have noticed that the planet Uranus is at the present time in a position leading the minds of men to think and reach out after spiritual causes, or a knowledge of the laws of life. Now the color of gold relates to the laws of life. Golden yellow, the base of spirituality, is in " sensation." In other words, sensation acts as the hand of the spirit, by means of which cognizance is had of material conditions, and people brought under the sway of the spirit.

On looking back over the history of our earth, we see how the mental conditions and tastes of humanity have been influenced by forms and images. Take, for example, a horse-shoe. People all now have a horse-shoe. They do not know the meaning, however, of what they have got. They have something really which has a magical power like Jacob's famous rods. Jacob made a bargain with Laban, his father-in-law (who had been in the habit of cheating him), that he, Jacob, was to have all the ring-streaked, the striped, and the speckled cattle as his personal reward, and Laban agreed. So Jacob peeled rods, that they might be alternately white, and set them in the water-trough, so that as the cattle drank they looked at those bright rods. And, behold! the cattle that were born were ring-streaked and speckled. That is an evidence of a law of Nature. The image of a thought presenting itself before the mind will impress itself upon the soul, the principle of which afterwards finds expression. Thus the world has been living up to the prophecies and carrying out the very things that were active in the great cause-mind a long time before. We are acting these out in our love for the principle of yellow. We are seeking rest; but the world is as yet finding little of it, I think.

We have said enough to enable the student to make up his combinations, and it will be unnecessary for me to go farther. If you have been enabled to hold the primates in your minds, you will be enabled to deduce, or induce, the colors that are made therefrom. You will see what are the combinations and what principle is expressed in a given color, which may be put before you. You now have a key to an unlimited variety of shades and colors. All there is for you to do is to study up a little as to what combinations and leading colors are in any particular shade, and then you will understand the mental conditions they express.

I want, by way of conclusion, to say a few words about the seven-pointed star as a geometrical figure. The laws of chemistry in Nature are expressed on this chart. Take the primary force and the second companion, discrimination, unite them as positive and negative, male and female, and the product invariably will be fermentation. The positive dominant principle that determines to hold and bind, and this discriminating principle that wants to get free from bondage and to act on its own account, represent, together, the strugglings of Nature in fermentation. The discriminating principle wants freedom, and obtains it only in fermentation. Let us take the next two, discrimination and order. The result of those conjoinedly is transmutation. In the case of the two principles, discrimination and order, discrimination struggles with the old order, and tries to inaugurate the new; and the action which is engendered by the two forces creates luminous potency, which is fire, and transmutative in its operation. Next, let us take order and cohesion. Here we have rest. The result is sensation. Here we have the perfectly organized man, with the divine mother acting within him and keeping all his parts cohering and working together in perfect harmony. How beautiful are the sensations and delights of such a life, if every part of the human being be perfect!

Take cohesion and fermentation. Those who indulge in intoxicating drinks know that the fermentation will master the strongest men. In these cases we have cohesion and fermentation united, and the result is like the force we find in an electric battery. Cohesion holds together, binds the atoms of metallic substances, and when we bring into contact with it the fermentative acid principle, which liberates the material qualities, force is the result. We are about to have our cars run. we are told, by electricity. The force of electricity is strong enough to run the world, and, as the greater includes the less, there is a certainty that electricity could run our railways.

Take transmutation, and here we see fermentation has done its work. An insect is born, and transmutation begins its work also; the grosser elements are thrown off, and a condition of discriminating and obtaining the right kind of food is the result of that work.

If we put transmutation and sensation together and add to the workings of transmutation the sense of right and wrong, which is the highest principle, we bring into activity the perfect law of order.

I have now gone around the diagram. As you possess a copy of this star, think it over; unite two adjacent points into their ultimate, and you will arrive at correct conclusions every time. The seven-pointed star will be the key to a wonderful system of chemistry in the not distant future; for seven is the perfection of all that is, though not of all that is to be. It is the perfection of physical nature.

www.ingramcontent.com/pod-product-compliance
Lightning Source LLC
Chambersburg PA
CBHW060513280326
41933CB00014B/2950